A Memory a Day for Moms

This Book Belongs To:

Name: _____

Address: _____

_____

_____

Phone Number: _____

E-mail Address: _____

I thank my God every time I remember you.

—PHILIPPIANS 1:3

A Memory a Day

FOR

Moms

Published in Nashville, Tennessee, by Thomas Nelson. Thomas Nelson is a registered trademark of HarperCollins Christian Publishing, Inc.

Thomas Nelson titles may be purchased in bulk for educational, business, fund-raising, or sales promotional use. For information, please e-mail SpecialMarkets@ThomasNelson.com.

Unless otherwise noted, Scripture quotations are taken from the Holy Bible, New International Version®, NIV®. Copyright © 1973, 1978, 1984, 2011 by Biblica, Inc.® Used by permission of Zondervan. All rights reserved worldwide. www.zondervan.com. The "NIV" and "New International Version" are trademarks registered in the United States Patent and Trademark Office by Biblica, Inc.®

Scripture quotations marked ESV are from the ESV® Bible (The Holy Bible, English Standard Version®). Copyright © 2001 by Crossway, a publishing ministry of Good News Publishers. Used by permission. All rights reserved.

Scripture quotations marked NASB are from the New American Standard Bible®, Copyright © 1960, 1962, 1963, 1968, 1971, 1972, 1973, 1975, 1977, 1995 by The Lockman Foundation. Used by permission. (www.Lockman.org)

Scripture quotations marked NKJV are from the New King James Version®. © 1982 by Thomas Nelson. Used by permission. All rights reserved.

Scripture quotations marked NLT are from the Holy Bible, New Living Translation. © 1996, 2004, 2007, 2013, 2015 by Tyndale House Foundation. Used by permission of Tyndale House Publishers, Inc., Carol Stream, Illinois 60188. All rights reserved.

Any Internet addresses, phone numbers, or company or product information printed in this book are offered as a resource and are not intended in any way to be or to imply an endorsement by Thomas Nelson, nor does Thomas Nelson vouch for the existence, content, or services of these sites, phone numbers, companies, or products beyond the life of this book.

Library of Congress Cataloging-in-Publication Data

ISBN 978-1-4003-1326-6 (HC)

Printed in China

18 19 20 21 22 TIMS 10 9 8 7 6 5 4 3 2 1

Introduction

Your relationship with your child and family is precious beyond measure. Yet in the whirlwind of life, small, special moments can easily be whisked away from your mind. Now, with the help of this guided journal, you can grasp those moments and turn them into a priceless bank of memories to keep and to share with the ones you love. Each day's entry is thoughtfully designed with a prompt, a selection of Scripture, and a prayer to help you take mindful snapshots of your time together, whether it's in a short sentence or a longer reflection. As you return to it each day, you'll find yourself becoming more present and thankful for the life God has given you to nurture.

What is your family's verse for this year?

1
January

20___ _____

20___ _____

20___ _____

20___ _____

20___ _____

We will not hide these truths from our children; we will tell the next generation about the glorious deeds of the LORD, about his power and his mighty wonders. —Psalm 78:4 NLT

Father, I pray that Your Word would be the compass by which our family navigates this next year.

2
January

What are your dreams for your child this year?

20 ___

20 ___

20 ___

20 ___

20 ___

"For I know the plans I have for you," declares the LORD, "plans to prosper you and not to harm you, plans to give you hope and a future." —Jeremiah 29:11

Lord God, direct our footsteps as a family this year, that every path we take shall bring glory to You.

What one thing does your child
want to learn this year?

3
January

20____ _____

_____

_____

20____ _____

_____

_____

20____ _____

_____

_____

20____ _____

_____

_____

20____ _____

_____

_____

Teach them his decrees and instructions, and show them the way
they are to live and how they are to behave. —Exodus 18:20

Father, teach me to love my child well,
as You have loved me perfectly.

4
January

*Your kids will only be this age once! What
will you miss most about this stage?*

20 ___ _____

20 ___ _____

20 ___ _____

20 ___ _____

20 ___ _____

*Every good and perfect gift is from above, coming down
from the Father of the heavenly lights. —James 1:17*

**Thank You, God, for the gift of loving this child, and
let me never forget the joy of being a mother.**

What word of encouragement do you
want to give to your child today?

5

January

20_____ _____

20_____ _____

20_____ _____

20_____ _____

20_____ _____

Therefore encourage one another and build one another up,
just as you are doing. —1 Thessalonians 5:11 ESV

God, let Your words be on my tongue today so that I can
speak only encouragement and love to my child.

6

January

What's the most meaningful thing your spouse does to support you in your role as mom?

20 ___ _____

20 ___ _____

20 ___ _____

20 ___ _____

20 ___ _____

We know that for those who love God all things work together for good, for those who are called according to his purpose. —Romans 8:28 ESV

Thank You, Father, for the people You have put in my life to support me. Through them, I see Your love for me.

*Before the day is over, what's one
thing you want to be sure to do?*

7

January

20___ _____

_____

_____

_____

20___ _____

_____

_____

_____

20___ _____

_____

_____

_____

20___ _____

_____

_____

_____

20___ _____

_____

_____

_____

*From the rising of the sun to the place where it sets, the
name of the LORD is to be praised. —Psalm 113:3*

**God, give me focus as I do the tasks on my to-do list
today so that I can make time to enjoy my child.**

8
January

What is your child's favorite song?

20 ___

20 ___

20 ___

20 ___

20 ___

Sing to the LORD a new song; sing to the LORD, all the earth.
Sing to the LORD, praise his name. —Psalm 96:1–2

Put Your song in my mind today, Lord, so words of praise
are always present in my mind. Let me sing to You!

What lesson does your child need to learn right now?

20 _____ _____

_____

_____

_____

20 _____ _____

_____

_____

_____

20 _____ _____

_____

_____

_____

20 _____ _____

_____

_____

_____

20 _____ _____

_____

_____

_____

My child, listen to what I say, and treasure my commands. —Proverbs 2:1 NLT

Father, remind me of the ways You are patient with me, and give me patience with my child as they learn so much about what it means to be responsible every day.

10
January

My child's personality is best described as _____.

20____ _____
_____
_____
_____

20____ _____
_____
_____
_____

20____ _____
_____
_____
_____

20____ _____
_____
_____
_____

20____ _____
_____
_____
_____

You . . . knit me together in my mother's womb. —Psalm 139:13 NLT

Lord, I praise You for the way You've created my child to be unique. Thank You for the delight of knowing them.

Who is your child's best friend?

20 _____ _____

_____

_____

_____

20 _____ _____

_____

_____

_____

20 _____ _____

_____

_____

_____

20 _____ _____

_____

_____

_____

20 _____ _____

_____

_____

_____

*A man of many companions may come to ruin, but there is a
friend who sticks closer than a brother.* —Proverbs 18:24 ESV

**God, as my child grows over the years, give them
wisdom as they choose their friends. Let them
be drawn to others who love You deeply.**

12
January

20___

20___

20___

20___

20___

"The LORD, the LORD, a God merciful and gracious, slow to anger, and abounding in steadfast love and faithfulness." —Exodus 34:6 ESV

Heavenly Father, thank You for the million different ways we're able to say I love you to each other, and help me find new ones each day.

*What is your favorite meal to cook
(or order in) for your family?*

13
January

20 ___ _____

_____

_____

_____

20 ___ _____

_____

_____

_____

20 ___ _____

_____

_____

_____

20 ___ _____

_____

_____

_____

20 ___ _____

_____

_____

_____

*Then all the people went away to eat and drink, to send portions of
food and to celebrate with great joy, because they now understood
the words that had been made known to them. —Nehemiah 8:12*

**Thank You for allowing us to celebrate Your goodness
and glory with the richness of good food.**

14
January

Who, outside your family, is loving your child well right now?

20 _____ _____

_____

_____

_____

20 _____ _____

_____

_____

_____

20 _____ _____

_____

_____

_____

20 _____ _____

_____

_____

_____

20 _____ _____

_____

_____

_____

"Let the little children come to me, and do not hinder them, for the kingdom of God belongs to such as these." —Luke 18:16

Lord, thank You for the friends and family members who love us well. I certainly couldn't do this all on my own!

What is your child's biggest fear?

20____ _____

20____ _____

20____ _____

20____ _____

20____ _____

"As one whom his mother comforts, so I will comfort you." —Isaiah 66:13 ESV

Wrap my child in the comfort of Your arms whenever they are afraid, Lord. Remind us both that You have us tightly in Your grip.

16

January

20 _____ _____

_____

_____

_____

20 _____ _____

_____

_____

_____

20 _____ _____

_____

_____

_____

20 _____ _____

_____

_____

_____

20 _____ _____

_____

_____

_____

*Grandchildren are the crowning glory of the aged; parents
are the pride of their children.* —Proverbs 17:6 NLT

**Father, thank You for leading my child down
the path You've chosen just for them, and help
me to recognize You in all they do.**

Has your child said something hilarious lately? Write it down!

17
January

20___ _____
_____
_____

20___ _____
_____
_____

20___ _____
_____
_____

20___ _____
_____
_____

20___ _____
_____
_____

He will once again fill your mouth with laughter and your lips with shouts of joy. —Job 8:21 NLT

God, I love to imagine You laughing with joy over the silly, strange things my child says or does. Thank You for the fun in the midst of the work of parenting.

18
January

What is your child's favorite book?

20 ___ _____

_____

_____

_____

20 ___ _____

_____

_____

_____

20 ___ _____

_____

_____

_____

20 ___ _____

_____

_____

_____

20 ___ _____

_____

_____

_____

Delight yourself in the LORD, and he will give you the desires of your heart. —Psalm 37:4 ESV

Lord, please give me a love for Your Word that spills over into my relationship with my child.

What three characteristics would
you like to develop as a mom?

20 _____ _____

20 _____ _____

20 _____ _____

20 _____ _____

20 _____ _____

The fruit of the Spirit is love, joy, peace, patience, kindness,
goodness, faithfulness, gentleness, self-control; against
such things there is no law. —Galatians 5:22–23 ESV

Father, grow Your fruit in me, so that my kid will
recognize them in every interaction with me.

20

January

How do you want your kid to describe you?

20 ___

20 ___

20 ___

20 ___

20 ___

She speaks with wisdom, and faithful instruction is on her tongue. She watches over the affairs of her household and does not eat the bread of idleness. —Proverbs 31:26–27

Father, please show my kid how much You love them through their relationship with me and their father.

What do you love about your home right now?

21
January

20___ _____

_____

_____

_____

20___ _____

_____

_____

_____

20___ _____

_____

_____

_____

20___ _____

_____

_____

_____

20___ _____

_____

_____

_____

As for me and my household, we will serve the Lord. —Joshua 24:15

Lord, protect me from complaining about the mess in my house or the things I wish I had, and instead focus on the amazing gift of the child You've given me to raise.

22

January

20 ___ _____

_____

_____

_____

20 ___ _____

_____

_____

_____

20 ___ _____

_____

_____

_____

20 ___ _____

_____

_____

_____

20 ___ _____

_____

_____

_____

God is greater than our feelings, and he knows everything. —1 John 3:20 NLT

Lord, help me recognize my emotions and deal with them, but not let them control me.

What have you been putting off lately? Why?

23
January

20___ _____

_____

_____

20___ _____

_____

_____

20___ _____

_____

_____

20___ _____

_____

_____

20___ _____

_____

_____

I will hurry, without delay, to obey your commands. —Psalm 119:60 NLT

Forgive my procrastination, God, and give me the motivation I need to fulfill Your call on my life.

24

January

What is your child's bedtime routine?

20 _____ _____

_____

_____

_____

20 _____ _____

_____

_____

_____

20 _____ _____

_____

_____

_____

20 _____ _____

_____

_____

_____

20 _____ _____

_____

_____

_____

I lay down and slept, yet I woke up in safety, for the
LORD was watching over me. —Psalm 3:5 NLT

Lord, thank You for watching over my child day and
night. In Your perfect care, I know they will be safe.

*What fun, crazy thing do you want to
do with your child today?*

20 ___ _____

20 ___ _____

20 ___ _____

20 ___ _____

20 ___ _____

*Rejoice in the Lord always; again I will say,
rejoice.* —*Philippians 4:4* ESV

Remind me, Lord, that life isn't all about chores
and responsibilities, but that taking time to play
with my child is glorifying to You too.

26
January

As a mom, what do you need to let go of?

20 _____ _____

20 _____ _____

20 _____ _____

20 _____ _____

20 _____ _____

For freedom Christ has set us free; stand firm therefore, and
do not submit again to a yoke of slavery. —Galatians 5:1 ESV

Father, filter the nonessentials out of my
life, so all that's left are the things that really
matter—the things You want in my life.

What's the best advice you've been given about parenting lately?

27
January

20___ _____

_____

_____

_____

20___ _____

_____

_____

_____

20___ _____

_____

_____

_____

20___ _____

_____

_____

_____

20___ _____

_____

_____

_____

Train up a child in the way he should go; even when he is old he will not depart from it. —Proverbs 22:6 ESV

Father, lead me to women who love You and have walked this road of mothering before me, so I can turn to them for wisdom when parenting gets difficult.

28
January

What is your child's favorite movie?

20 ___

20 ___

20 ___

20 ___

20 ___

He brought me out into a broad place; he rescued me,
because he delighted in me. —Psalm 18:19 ESV

Lord, help me embrace the joy of the adventure
in life and pass that joy on to my child.

What's your favorite thing to do as a family?

29
January

20___

20___

20___

20___

20___

*Trust in the LORD and do good; dwell in the land
and enjoy safe pasture.* —Psalm 37:3

Father God, I ask that You would let harmony
and peace reign over our household, so our time
spent together is our favorite time.

30
January

How does your family make you feel loved?

20 ___ _____

20 ___ _____

20 ___ _____

20 ___ _____

20 ___ _____

Learn first of all to put their religion into practice by caring for their own family and so repaying their parents and grandparents, for this is pleasing to God. —1 Timothy 5:4

Please show me, Lord, the best way to show my husband and my child how much I love them.

What one thing can you not
live without these days?

31
January

20 ___ _____

_____

_____

_____

20 ___ _____

_____

_____

_____

20 ___ _____

_____

_____

_____

20 ___ _____

_____

_____

_____

20 ___ _____

_____

_____

_____

My God will meet all your needs according to the riches
of his glory in Christ Jesus. —Philippians 4:19

Remind me, Lord, that no matter what I may think I need
to get through the day, really all I will ever need is You.

1
February

In Scripture, what verse is speaking most meaningfully to you right now?

20____ _____

20____ _____

20____ _____

20____ _____

20____ _____

"Honor your father and mother." This is the first commandment with a promise: If you honor your father and mother, "things will go well for you, and you will have a long life on the earth." —Ephesians 6:2–3 NLT

Remind me every morning of Your unfailing love.

What fears do you have about motherhood?

20 _____ _____

20 _____ _____

20 _____ _____

20 _____ _____

20 _____ _____

My child, listen when your father corrects you. Don't neglect your mother's instruction. What you learn from them will crown you with grace and be a chain of honor around your neck. —Proverbs 1:8–9 NLT

Help me look at You when my fears creep in, so that I may focus on Your steady love instead of my unsteady emotions.

3
February

How could you make more room in your life for the things you love?

20 ___ _____

_____

_____

_____

20 ___ _____

_____

_____

_____

20 ___ _____

_____

_____

_____

20 ___ _____

_____

_____

_____

20 ___ _____

_____

_____

_____

A gracious woman gains respect, but ruthless men gain only wealth. —Proverbs 11:16 NLT

Father, give me wisdom as I plan for the spring and summer with my family. Help me commit us to the things we love and that glorify You, not those that drain the life out of us.

What inspires you as a mom?

4
February

20 _____ _____

_____

_____

_____

20 _____ _____

_____

_____

_____

20 _____ _____

_____

_____

_____

20 _____ _____

_____

_____

_____

20 _____ _____

_____

_____

_____

*The father of the righteous will greatly rejoice; he who fathers
a wise son will be glad in him. —Proverbs 23:24 ESV*

**God, thank You for beautiful moments in my life,
and help me appreciate them even more.**

5
February

Think back to your most joyful childhood memory. What is it?

20___ _____

_____

_____

_____

20___ _____

_____

_____

_____

20___ _____

_____

_____

_____

20___ _____

_____

_____

_____

20___ _____

_____

_____

_____

Above all, keep loving one another earnestly, since love covers a multitude of sins. —1 Peter 4:8 ESV

Father, gently direct my attitude to be one of joyful wonder, not to be hurried and frustrated, so that I can relive the joy of childhood again with my child.

Look at your calendar and schedule some time for just you—whether it's a weekend away or just a few hours. What will you do with your time?

6
February

20 _____

20 _____

20 _____

20 _____

20 _____

Take care, and keep your soul diligently, lest you forget the things that your eyes have seen. Make them known to your children and your children's children. —Deuteronomy 4:9 ESV

Father, thank You for the moments of solitude and restoration. Help me make the most of them.

7

February

What is your child's favorite game to play?

20____ _____

_____

_____

_____

20____ _____

_____

_____

_____

20____ _____

_____

_____

_____

20____ _____

_____

_____

_____

20____ _____

_____

_____

_____

The wisest of women builds her house, but folly with her own hands tears it down. —Proverbs 14:1 ESV

God, give me a playful spirit that shows my child how much I love to be with them.

Have you asked anyone for parenting advice recently? What did you ask?

8
February

20 ____ _____

_____

_____

_____

20 ____ _____

_____

_____

_____

20 ____ _____

_____

_____

_____

20 ____ _____

_____

_____

_____

20 ____ _____

_____

_____

_____

Blessed is everyone who fears the LORD, who walks in his ways! You shall eat the fruit of the labor of your hands; you shall be blessed, and it shall be well with you. —Psalm 128:1–2 ESV

Father, please bless my efforts as I try to parent my child well, and remind me of the truth I find in Your Word.

9

February

20 ___

20 ___

20 ___

20 ___

20 ___

My son, keep your father's command and do not forsake
your mother's teaching. Bind them always on your heart;
fasten them around your neck. —Proverbs 6:20–21

God, please give me the grace to laugh and enjoy
the chaos that children can cause.

Has your heart swelled with love for your child recently? What was happening at the time?

10
February

20____ _____

_____

_____

_____

20____ _____

_____

_____

_____

20____ _____

_____

_____

_____

20____ _____

_____

_____

_____

20____ _____

_____

_____

_____

My soul glorifies the Lord and my spirit rejoices in God my Savior, for he has been mindful of the humble state of his servant. From now on all generations will call me blessed. —Luke 1:46–48

God, my heart is so full of love for this tiny child. Help me appreciate every moment I have with them.

11
February

Describe a major mom win you've had recently.

20 ___ _____

20 ___ _____

20 ___ _____

20 ___ _____

20 ___ _____

Charm is deceptive, and beauty is fleeting; but a woman who fears the LORD is to be praised. —Proverbs 31:30

Father, thank You for moments that give me confidence as a mom, but remind me that all I accomplish is through Your grace.

Describe a major mom fail you've had recently.

12
February

20___ _____

_____

_____

_____

20___ _____

_____

_____

_____

20___ _____

_____

_____

_____

20___ _____

_____

_____

_____

20___ _____

_____

_____

_____

Her children stand and bless her. Her husband
praises her. —Proverbs 31:28 NLT

Holy Father, forgive me the many failures I have
as a woman and as a mother, and help me do better
so I can help my child see Your glory more.

13
February

My favorite restaurant for a date night with my child is _____.

20___ _____

20___ _____

20___ _____

20___ _____

20___ _____

She carefully watches everything in her household and suffers nothing from laziness. —Proverbs 31:27 NLT

God, thanks for the many blessings and abundances You've given me in life. Remind me that all I have is from You.

How will you show your child you love them today, on Valentine's Day?

14
February

20 ___ _____

_____

_____

_____

20 ___ _____

_____

_____

_____

20 ___ _____

_____

_____

_____

20 ___ _____

_____

_____

_____

20 ___ _____

_____

_____

_____

The LORD your God is living among you. He is a mighty savior. He will take delight in you with gladness. With his love, he will calm all your fears. He will rejoice over you with joyful songs. —Zephaniah 3:17 NLT

Father, today is all about love, so help me celebrate the great love I have for my child and my family today.

15
February

Is your family going on vacation this year? If so, where?

20 ___

20 ___

20 ___

20 ___

20 ___

He will command his angels concerning you to guard you in all your ways. —Psalm 91:11 ESV

God, it's so much fun to dream of the amazing places You created on this planet that I might be able to take my child to visit. Thank You for Your wonder and creativity.

*What three (or more) things do you
share in common with your child?*

16
February

20 ___ _____

_____

_____

20 ___ _____

_____

_____

20 ___ _____

_____

_____

20 ___ _____

_____

_____

20 ___ _____

_____

_____

*Let your father and mother be glad; let her who
bore you rejoice. —Proverbs 23:25 ESV*

**Father, this child You gave me is such a gift. Thank
You for giving me things to share in common
with them, which will connect us forever.**

17
February

What is your child's favorite place to visit?

20 ___ _____

_____

_____

_____

20 ___ _____

_____

_____

_____

20 ___ _____

_____

_____

_____

20 ___ _____

_____

_____

_____

20 ___ _____

_____

_____

_____

The promise of entering his rest still stands. —Hebrews 4:1 ESV

Lord, it's so easy to fall into the habit of work, work, work as a mom. Please, remind me to rest.

What do you worry about with your child?

20___ _____

_____

_____

20___ _____

_____

_____

20___ _____

_____

_____

20___ _____

_____

_____

20___ _____

_____

_____

_____

Perfect love expels all fear. —1 John 4:18 NLT

Lord God, take my fears and toss them far away. Replace them with perfect trust and love for You.

19
February

If you could do anything on a dream date night with your husband, what would it be?

20 ___ _____

_____

_____

_____

20 ___ _____

_____

_____

_____

20 ___ _____

_____

_____

_____

20 ___ _____

_____

_____

_____

20 ___ _____

_____

_____

_____

In fact God has placed the parts in the body, every one of them, just as he wanted them to be. —1 Corinthians 12:18

Father, remind me to pursue a deeper and more exciting relationship with my spouse every day. The gift of that relationship is one I don't want to take for granted.

*What advice do you have for other
moms of kids your child's age?*

20
February

20 _____ _____

20 _____ _____

20 _____ _____

20 _____ _____

20 _____ _____

*He said to me, "My grace is sufficient for you, for my power
is made perfect in weakness." —2 Corinthians 12:9*

**God, help me to be always learning as a mom. Let
me be eager to listen and slow to speak.**

21
February

What is your child's cutest feature?

20___

20___

20___

20___

20___

I praise you because I am fearfully and wonderfully made; your works are wonderful, I know that full well. —Psalm 139:14

God, I delight in the child You have given me. Thank You for such an adorable, lovable gift.

What traditions do you want to
create with your family?

22
February

20_____ _____

20_____ _____

20_____ _____

20_____ _____

20_____ _____

*"Never! Can a mother forget her nursing child? . . . But even if
that were possible, I would not forget you!" —Isaiah 49:15 NLT*

**Father, help me to be intentional about the traditions
my family starts. Let us make them meaningful
and centered on You and Your glory.**

23
February

20 _____

20 _____

20 _____

20 _____

20 _____

For God is working in you, giving you the desire and the
power to do what pleases him. —Philippians 2:13 NLT

Lord, help me to always do what pleases You. Of
course, I know it's impossible since I'm far from
perfect. But that is the desire of my heart.

What would you like to change about your home?

24
February

20___ _____

20___ _____

20___ _____

20___ _____

20___ _____

A wise woman builds her home, but a foolish woman tears it down with her own hands. —Proverbs 14:1 NLT

Father, I pray that my house is a place of hospitality, where those who need love and comfort would find friendship, peace, and acceptance.

25
February

What is your favorite way to spend the day?

20___

20___

20___

20___

20___

Let your requests be made known to God. And the peace of God, which surpasses all understanding, will guard your hearts and your minds in Christ Jesus. —Philippians 4:6–7 ESV

God, this is the day You have made for me. Help me find You in all the details of it.

What do you wish others knew
about you? About your child?

26
February

20____ _____

_____

_____

_____

20____ _____

_____

_____

_____

20____ _____

_____

_____

_____

20____ _____

_____

_____

_____

20____ _____

_____

_____

_____

*Remembering before our God and Father your work
of faith and labor of love and steadfastness of hope in
our Lord Jesus Christ. —1 Thessalonians 1:3 ESV*

**God, it's my desire to be known and loved. Help me find those
friends who would love me, and teach me to love other people.**

27
February

What is your child's favorite toy?

20___ _____
_____
_____
_____

20___ _____
_____
_____
_____

20___ _____
_____
_____
_____

20___ _____
_____
_____
_____

20___ _____
_____
_____
_____

For everything there is a season, and a time for every matter under heaven. —Ecclesiastes 3:1 ESV

Father, my child is growing so quickly and their interests are changing so fast. Help me enjoy each and every stage of their childhood.

*Memories fade fast, so what one thing
do you always want to remember about
this phase of your child's life?*

28
February

20 _____ _____

_____

_____

_____

20 _____ _____

_____

_____

_____

20 _____ _____

_____

_____

_____

20 _____ _____

_____

_____

_____

20 _____ _____

_____

_____

_____

*Who knows if perhaps you were made . . . for just
such a time as this?* —Esther 4:14 NLT

**Father, help me remember the great moments in my
child's life, but also appreciate the hard phases too; and
remember that You walked with me through both.**

29
February

Leap Year comes around nearly every four years. If this is one of those years, what did you and your child do with the extra day?

20 ___ _____

_____

_____

_____

20 ___ _____

_____

_____

_____

20 ___ _____

_____

_____

_____

20 ___ _____

_____

_____

_____

20 ___ _____

_____

_____

_____

Teach us to number our days, that we may present to You a heart of wisdom. —Psalm 90:12 NASB

Only You know how many days each of our lives hold. Help me to manage the time You give wisely and to cherish each day I'm given as a mother.

What hard thing has your child
accomplished recently?

1
March

20___ _____

_____

_____

_____

20___ _____

_____

_____

_____

20___ _____

_____

_____

_____

20___ _____

_____

_____

_____

20___ _____

_____

_____

_____

God is not unjust; he will not forget your work and
the love you have shown him. —Hebrews 6:10

Father, it's hard to watch my child struggle. Remind me
that I can't do everything for them, and that sometimes
learning the hard way is the best way to remember.

2
March

20 ___ _____

_____

_____

_____

20 ___ _____

_____

_____

_____

20 ___ _____

_____

_____

_____

20 ___ _____

_____

_____

_____

20 ___ _____

_____

_____

_____

*"Come to me, all you who are weary and burdened,
and I will give you rest." —Matthew 11:28*

**God, motherhood isn't always easy. Give me
grace to get through the hard times.**

What are you hopeful about?

20____ _____

20____ _____

20____ _____

20____ _____

20____ _____

Those who hope in the LORD will renew their strength. They will soar on wings like eagles; they will run and not grow weary, they will walk and not be faint. —Isaiah 40:31

You give me a hope and a future, Lord. Remind me of the hope I have in You every day.

4

March

20 ___ _____
_____
_____
_____

20 ___ _____
_____
_____
_____

20 ___ _____
_____
_____
_____

20 ___ _____
_____
_____
_____

20 ___ _____
_____
_____
_____

Let all that I am wait quietly before God, for my hope is in him.
He alone is my rock and my salvation. —Psalm 62:5–6 NLT

God, I never knew the ways my child would change
me—and maybe that's a good thing! As I grow and
learn, let my heart always be tied to You.

What's your biggest parenting trial right now?

5
March

20___ _____

_____

_____

_____

20___ _____

_____

_____

_____

20___ _____

_____

_____

_____

20___ _____

_____

_____

_____

20___ _____

_____

_____

_____

*When troubles of any kind come your way, consider
it an opportunity for great joy. —James 1:2 NLT*

**Father God, I'm struggling with certain parts
of parenting right now. Make Your will clear
to me, and help me follow Your plan.**

6
March

What has your child taught you about God's character recently?

20 ___ _____

_____

_____

20 ___ _____

_____

_____

20 ___ _____

_____

_____

20 ___ _____

_____

_____

20 ___ _____

_____

_____

Let [your body] be a living and holy sacrifice—the kind he will find acceptable. This is truly the way to worship him. —Romans 12:1 NLT

God, I give all of myself—physically, emotionally, and mentally—to my child some days. Help me seek my rest and restoration in You.

What's your biggest worry?

20 ___ _____

_____

_____

_____

20 ___ _____

_____

_____

_____

20 ___ _____

_____

_____

_____

20 ___ _____

_____

_____

_____

20 ___ _____

_____

_____

_____

"Be still, and know that I am God. I will be exalted among the nations, I will be exalted in the earth!" —Psalm 46:10 ESV

God, I give my family over to You. I know I will probably always worry and fret over them, but I also trust You have them firmly in Your protective grip.

8
March

What's your favorite memory with your child?

20____ _____

20____ _____

20____ _____

20____ _____

20____ _____

Remember the wondrous works that he has done, his miracles and the judgments he uttered. —1 Chronicles 16:12 ESV

God, You have done amazing things in the life of my child. Please continue to work in them for Your glory.

What is your child's favorite thing about you?

9
March

20___ _____

20___ _____

20___ _____

20___ _____

20___ _____

She opens her mouth with wisdom, and the teaching of kindness is on her tongue. —Proverbs 31:26 ESV

Father God, I pray that You will put a hedge of protection around my relationship with my child, so that they will always love and respect their time with me.

10
March

Of all the things you do for your child,
what's your favorite mothering task?

20 ___ _____

_____

_____

20 ___ _____

_____

_____

20 ___ _____

_____

_____

20 ___ _____

_____

_____

20 ___ _____

_____

_____

Work willingly at whatever you do, as though you were working
for the Lord rather than for people. —Colossians 3:23 NLT

Father, mothering is hard work, but it is also the
joy of my life. Thank You for the opportunity
to serve You and my child in this role.

*What's the silliest thing you've
done with your child lately?*

11
March

20 _____ _____

_____

_____

20 _____ _____

_____

_____

20 _____ _____

_____

_____

20 _____ _____

_____

_____

20 _____ _____

_____

_____

*Don't try to impress others. Be humble, thinking of others
as better than yourselves. —Philippians 2:3 NLT*

**God, give me the freedom to let loose with my child and
have fun on occasion. Fill our home with joy.**

12
March

My favorite thing about being a mom
is _____.

20 ___ _____

20 ___ _____

20 ___ _____

20 ___ _____

20 ___ _____

*Trust in the LORD with all your heart and lean not
on your own understanding.* —Proverbs 3:5

God, I don't always know what I'm doing when it
comes to motherhood, but I trust Your ways and
Your plan for me. Thank You for loving me.

What is your child's greatest strength?

13
March

20___ _____

20___ _____

20___ _____

20___ _____

20___ _____

Do everything without grumbling or arguing, so that you may become blameless and pure. —Philippians 2:14–15

Lord, I pray that my child will grow to become a shining light for You. That anyone who knows them will know, without a doubt, they are a child of God.

14
March

What is your child's love language, and how do you show it to them at this age?

20 ___ _____

_____

_____

_____

20 ___ _____

_____

_____

_____

20 ___ _____

_____

_____

_____

20 ___ _____

_____

_____

_____

20 ___ _____

_____

_____

_____

You have searched me, LORD, and you know me. You know when I sit and when I rise; you perceive my thoughts from afar. —Psalm 139:1–2

God, help me love my child well in the specific ways they need it right now.

What have you done recently, that you would have never thought you could do before becoming a mom?

15
March

20___ _____

_____

_____

_____

20___ _____

_____

_____

_____

20___ _____

_____

_____

_____

20___ _____

_____

_____

_____

20___ _____

_____

_____

_____

As the Scriptures say, "I will destroy the wisdom of the wise and discard the intelligence of the intelligent. —1 Corinthians 1:19 NLT

God, remind me every day that Your thoughts are better than my thoughts. Help me turn to You and Your Word, instead of my own wisdom, as I raise this child.

16
March

20 _____

20 _____

20 _____

20 _____

20 _____

He gives power to the weak and strength to
the powerless. —Isaiah 40:29 NLT

Father, at times I feel almost faint with the
exhaustion of parenting. Give me Your strength
to make it through the tiring days.

Are you planning a vacation anywhere exciting, even if it's only on a Pinterest board and not in real life?

17
March

20 ___ _____

_____

_____

_____

20 ___ _____

_____

_____

_____

20 ___ _____

_____

_____

_____

20 ___ _____

_____

_____

_____

20 ___ _____

_____

_____

_____

O LORD, do not stay far away! You are my strength; come quickly to my aid! —Psalm 22:19 NLT

God, thank You for always being near. Remind me of Your presence when I start to feel weary.

18
March

The biggest parenting lie I've told is . . .

20 ____ _____

20 ____ _____

20 ____ _____

20 ____ _____

20 ____ _____

"Before I formed you in the womb I knew you, and before you were born I consecrated you." —Jeremiah 1:5 ESV

God, You have known my child longer than I have. Thank You for creating this little one just the way You desired.

What is your child wishing for most right now?

19
March

20___ _____

20___ _____

20___ _____

20___ _____

20___ _____

*"Ask, and it will be given to you; seek, and you will find; knock,
and it will be opened to you."* —Matthew 7:7 ESV

**God, please give my child a love for You so deep that
anything they desire would be from You.**

20

March

The craziest thing I've done for my child is . . .

20 __ _____

20 __ _____

20 __ _____

20 __ _____

20 __ _____

*"Have I not commanded you? Be strong and courageous.
Do not be frightened, and do not be dismayed, for the LORD
your God is with you wherever you go." —Joshua 1:9 ESV*

**Father, thank You for reminding me that I can handle
anything You send my way—even the craziest of kid antics.**

*When the house is finally quiet for
the night, what do you do?*

21

March

20___ —————————————————————————————

————————————————————————————————————

————————————————————————————————————

————————————————————————————————————

20___ —————————————————————————————

————————————————————————————————————

————————————————————————————————————

————————————————————————————————————

20___ —————————————————————————————

————————————————————————————————————

————————————————————————————————————

————————————————————————————————————

20___ —————————————————————————————

————————————————————————————————————

————————————————————————————————————

————————————————————————————————————

20___ —————————————————————————————

————————————————————————————————————

————————————————————————————————————

————————————————————————————————————

*But as for you, be strong and do not give up, for your
work will be rewarded. —2 Chronicles 15:7*

**Father, when I'm tempted to go hide in the bathroom
to get away from the stress of motherhood,
remind me that this verse is true.**

22
March

The most fun I've had as a parent recently was when _____.

20___ _____

_____

_____

_____

20___ _____

_____

_____

_____

20___ _____

_____

_____

_____

20___ _____

_____

_____

_____

20___ _____

_____

_____

_____

The LORD is my shepherd, I lack nothing. He makes me lie down in green pastures, he leads me beside quiet waters, he refreshes my soul. —Psalm 23:1–3

Father, thank You for the fun memories I'm making with my child, and remind me to return to You for refreshment each day.

What are you looking forward to
this spring with your kids?

23
March

20 _____

20 _____

20 _____

20 _____

20 _____

From the ends of the earth I call to you, I call as my heart grows
faint; lead me to the rock that is higher than I. —Psalm 61:2

Lord God, You are my rock and my refuge. Lead
me to You whenever I get tired.

24
March

20 _____ _____

_____

_____

_____

20 _____ _____

_____

_____

_____

20 _____ _____

_____

_____

_____

20 _____ _____

_____

_____

_____

20 _____ _____

_____

_____

_____

God is our refuge and strength, always ready to help in times of trouble. —Psalm 46:1 NLT

God, give me an adventuresome spirit to try new things and explore Your world with my child, remembering that You are always my refuge.

What other mom—celebrity or totally
average—inspires you today?

25
March

20____ _____

_____

_____

_____

20____ _____

_____

_____

_____

20____ _____

_____

_____

_____

20____ _____

_____

_____

_____

20____ _____

_____

_____

_____

*This I declare about the LORD: He alone is my refuge, my place
of safety; he is my God, and I trust him. —Psalm 91:2 NLT*

**God, help me let go of the things I rely on to get me
through the day, and instead turn to You as my everything.**

26

March

My biggest pet peeves about my kid's current
stage of life is _____.

20___ _____

20___ _____

20___ _____

20___ _____

20___ _____

When I am afraid, I will put my trust in you. —Psalm 56:3 NLT

**Father, when little, unimportant things bother
me, it's a sign that I'm not resting in You. Bring
me back to You whenever I drift away.**

The TV show I'm binging on right now is _____.

20___ _____

_____

_____

20___ _____

_____

_____

20___ _____

_____

_____

20___ _____

_____

_____

20___ _____

_____

_____

When doubts filled my mind, your comfort gave me renewed hope and cheer. —Psalm 94:19 NLT

Oh, Father, parenting is hard. But You are good. When I feel like I'm losing control, remind me that You've been in control the whole time.

28
March

20___ _____

_____

_____

_____

20___ _____

_____

_____

_____

20___ _____

_____

_____

_____

20___ _____

_____

_____

_____

20___ _____

_____

_____

_____

Fearing people is a dangerous trap, but trusting the
LORD means safety. —Proverbs 29:25 NLT

Lord, protect me from the trap of worrying about what
other mothers think of me. Your opinion is all that matters.

What is your child's favorite animal?

29
March

20___ _____

_____

_____

20___ _____

_____

_____

20___ _____

_____

_____

20___ _____

_____

_____

20___ _____

_____

_____

You keep him in perfect peace whose mind is stayed on you, because he trusts in you. —Isaiah 26:3 ESV

Father, my mind is so busy with thoughts of things I need to do. Please calm me with Your peace and remind me to trust You.

30
March

Ugh, I get so angry in parenting when _____.

20___ _____
_____
_____
_____

20___ _____
_____
_____
_____

20___ _____
_____
_____
_____

20___ _____
_____
_____
_____

20___ _____
_____
_____
_____

*The LORD is near to the brokenhearted and saves
the crushed in spirit. —Psalm 34:18 ESV*

**Father, You know those who are heavy on my heart because
they're hurting. Thank You for Your promise to save them.**

My favorite part about Sunday mornings
is _____.

31
March

20____ _____

_____

_____

20____ _____

_____

_____

20____ _____

_____

_____

20____ _____

_____

_____

20____ _____

_____

_____

*The steadfast love of the LORD never ceases; his mercies
never come to an end.* —Lamentations 3:22 ESV

**Father, Your mercies are new every morning.
Great is Your faithfulness!**

1
April

*What April Fool's joke do you plan
to play on your child, if any?*

20____ _____
_____
_____
_____

20____ _____
_____
_____
_____

20____ _____
_____
_____
_____

20____ _____
_____
_____
_____

20____ _____
_____
_____
_____

*I consider that our present sufferings are not worth comparing
with the glory that will be revealed in us.* —Romans 8:18

**God, give me a vision for the glory You have
planned for me and for my family.**

What does your child want to
be when they grow up?

2
April

20 _____ _____

_____

_____

_____

20 _____ _____

_____

_____

_____

20 _____ _____

_____

_____

_____

20 _____ _____

_____

_____

_____

20 _____ _____

_____

_____

_____

Let the Spirit renew your thoughts and attitudes. —Ephesians 4:23 NLT

**Father, I long for my thoughts to be captivated
by You and the things of You alone.**

3
April

What is your favorite Easter tradition?

20____ _____

_____

_____

_____

20____ _____

_____

_____

_____

20____ _____

_____

_____

_____

20____ _____

_____

_____

_____

20____ _____

_____

_____

_____

According to his great mercy, he has caused us to be born again to a living hope through the resurrection of Jesus Christ from the dead. —1 Peter 1:3 ESV

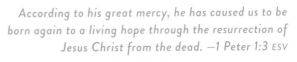

In You, Lord, I have hope! I pray that Your light in this world will grow ever brighter.

How do you plan to celebrate Easter this year?

4
April

20___ _____

_____

_____

_____

20___ _____

_____

_____

_____

20___ _____

_____

_____

_____

20___ _____

_____

_____

_____

20___ _____

_____

_____

_____

We do not lose heart. . . . For the things that are seen are transient, but the things that are unseen are eternal. —2 Corinthians 4:16, 18 ESV

God, dirty diapers and teething gums are not going to last forever. Remind me of this, and help me focus on You when I get discouraged.

5
April

What do you love most about that adorable kid of yours right now?

20 ___ _____

20 ___ _____

20 ___ _____

20 ___ _____

20 ___ _____

I lift up my eyes to the mountains—where does my help come from? My help comes from the LORD, the Maker of heaven and earth. He will not let your foot slip—he who watches over you will not slumber. —Psalm 121:1–3

Oh, Lord, I'm so in love with this child. Let that love spill over into every aspect of my relationship with them.

What is your wildest dream for your child?

6

April

20____ _____

_____

_____

_____

20____ _____

_____

_____

_____

20____ _____

_____

_____

_____

20____ _____

_____

_____

_____

20____ _____

_____

_____

_____

"Don't be afraid, for I am with you. Don't be discouraged, for I am your God. I will strengthen you and help you. I will hold you up with my victorious right hand." —Isaiah 41:10 NLT

Father, mold my child so their dreams are aligned with Your will and purposes for their life.

7

April

20 ___ _____

_____

_____

_____

20 ___ _____

_____

_____

_____

20 ___ _____

_____

_____

_____

20 ___ _____

_____

_____

_____

20 ___ _____

_____

_____

_____

Let all that I am wait quietly before God, for
my hope is in him. —Psalm 62:5 NLT

Lord God, as much as I enjoy the dreams I have
for my child, I recognize there is nothing so good
in my life as the plans You have for me.

What does your child do that makes you laugh?

8
April

20___ _____

20___ _____

20___ _____

20___ _____

20___ _____

Prepare your minds for action and exercise self-control. Put all your hope in the gracious salvation that will come to you when Jesus Christ is revealed to the world. —1 Peter 1:13 NLT

Thank You, God, for the joy of laughing with my child. Let that delight fill our house daily.

9
April

How do you want your child to make a difference in the world?

20 ___ _____

_____

_____

_____

20 ___ _____

_____

_____

_____

20 ___ _____

_____

_____

_____

20 ___ _____

_____

_____

_____

20 ___ _____

_____

_____

_____

Finally, brothers, whatever is true, whatever is honorable,
. . . if there is any excellence, if there is anything worthy of
praise, think about these things. —Philippians 4:8 ESV

Father, I hope I can leave this world a better place than I
found it, and that I can teach my child to do the same.

What's your favorite quirk about your child?

10
April

20 _____

20 _____

20 _____

20 _____

20 _____

*Count it all joy, my brothers, when you meet trials of
various kinds, for you know that the testing of your
faith produces steadfastness. —James 1:2–3 ESV*

**Heavenly Father, let my child always be exactly who
You designed them to be—quirks and all.**

11
April

How has your child shown kindness this week?

20____ _____

20____ _____

20____ _____

20____ _____

20____ _____

A joyful heart is good medicine, but a crushed spirit dries up the bones. —Proverbs 17:22 ESV

Father, I pray that my child will always be drawn to kindness and compassion in others.

*What's the newest parenting trend
in the media this week?*

12
April

20 ___ _____

_____

_____

20 ___ _____

_____

_____

20 ___ _____

_____

_____

20 ___ _____

_____

_____

20 ___ _____

_____

_____

*Do not conform to the pattern of this world, but be transformed by the
renewing of your mind. Then you will be able to test and approve what
God's will is—his good, pleasing and perfect will. —Romans 12:2*

**God, don't let me be swayed by the constantly changing patterns
in society but be anchored by the truth of Your Word.**

13
April

*How do you hope to leave the world
better for your child's generation?*

20 ___ _____

_____

_____

_____

20 ___ _____

_____

_____

_____

20 ___ _____

_____

_____

_____

20 ___ _____

_____

_____

_____

20 ___ _____

_____

_____

_____

*When he saw the crowds, he had compassion on them, because they were
harassed and helpless, like sheep without a shepherd.* —Matthew 9:36

**God, please give me eyes to see the world as You see it, and to
be a source of compassion and comfort to those in need.**

What new skill did your child learn recently?

14
April

20___ _____

_____

_____

20___ _____

_____

_____

20___ _____

_____

_____

20___ _____

_____

_____

20___ _____

_____

_____

You make known to me the path of life; you will fill me with joy in your presence, with eternal pleasures at your right hand. —Psalm 16:11

God, the glories You have planned for us are so exciting. I cannot wait to experience the fullness of Your presence.

15
April

Today I'm going to get out of my comfort zone and let my child _____.

20 ___ _____

_____

_____

_____

20 ___ _____

_____

_____

_____

20 ___ _____

_____

_____

_____

20 ___ _____

_____

_____

_____

20 ___ _____

_____

_____

_____

"You will live in joy and peace. The mountains and hills will burst into song, and the trees of the field will clap their hands!" —Isaiah 55:12 NLT

Father, it can be scary to let go and try new things—especially when it comes to my child. Give me courage to trust in You.

*In what ways are you tempted
to "give in" as a mom?*

16
April

20___ _____

_____

_____

_____

20___ _____

_____

_____

_____

20___ _____

_____

_____

_____

20___ _____

_____

_____

_____

20___ _____

_____

_____

_____

*We destroy every proud obstacle that keeps people
from knowing God.* —2 Corinthians 10:5 NLT

**Father, occasionally I'm reminded that I'm in a battle
for my child's soul to know You. Give me strength to
stay strong and fight for what is right and good.**

17
April

How do you feel the need to protect your child?

20___ _____

_____

_____

_____

20___ _____

_____

_____

_____

20___ _____

_____

_____

_____

20___ _____

_____

_____

_____

20___ _____

_____

_____

_____

For your royal husband delights in your beauty; honor him, for he is your lord. —Psalm 45:11 NLT

Lord, thank You for the reminder that You find me beautiful. Help me to be faithful to You always.

*What is your favorite recent memory
you've made with your child?*

18
April

20 _____ _____

_____

_____

_____

20 _____ _____

_____

_____

_____

20 _____ _____

_____

_____

_____

20 _____ _____

_____

_____

_____

20 _____ _____

_____

_____

_____

*You made all the delicate, inner parts of my body and knit
me together in my mother's womb. —Psalm 139:13 NLT*

**Creator God, You made my child perfectly,
and I praise You for that.**

19
April

How is God drawing you to Himself this week?

20 ___ _____

_____

_____

_____

20 ___ _____

_____

_____

_____

20 ___ _____

_____

_____

_____

20 ___ _____

_____

_____

_____

20 ___ _____

_____

_____

_____

"I have loved you, my people, with an everlasting love. With unfailing love I have drawn you to myself." —Jeremiah 31:3 NLT

Father, please continue to draw me closer to You. Never, ever, ever let me go.

What creative project are you inspired to do this week, maybe even with your child (if you dare)?

20
April

20____ _____

_____

_____

_____

20____ _____

_____

_____

_____

20____ _____

_____

_____

_____

20____ _____

_____

_____

_____

20____ _____

_____

_____

_____

*For we are his workmanship, created in Christ Jesus
for good works, which God prepared beforehand, that
we should walk in them. —Ephesians 2:10 ESV*

**God, I'm inspired by Your creativity. Please
increase that in me and my child too.**

21
April

How have you seen God's love at work in your life this week?

20____

20____

20____

20____

20____

So that Christ may dwell in your hearts through faith . . . to know the love of Christ that surpasses knowledge, that you may be filled with all the fullness of God. —Ephesians 3:17–19 ESV

God, I praise You for Your deep, deep love. May it be something I know and recognize more and more every day.

*Who or what is bringing light and
joy into your life right now?*

22
April

20 ___ _____

_____

_____

20 ___ _____

_____

_____

20 ___ _____

_____

_____

20 ___ _____

_____

_____

20 ___ _____

_____

_____

*Those who are wise shall shine like the brightness of the
sky above; and those who turn many to righteousness,
like the stars forever and ever. —Daniel 12:3 ESV*

**Father, help me to be a light that reflects You to others
in my life—including my child—this week.**

23
April

Are you happy with your level of fitness or exercise right now? If not, what can you do to change that?

20___ _____

20___ _____

20___ _____

20___ _____

20___ _____

You were bought at a price. Therefore honor God with your bodies. —1 Corinthians 6:20

God, my body belongs to You, but I often fail to treat it that way. Remind me that I am a temple for You, and let that inspire the decisions I make.

What is the strangest thing you've told
your child not to do recently?

24
April

20 _____ _____

_____

_____

_____

20 _____ _____

_____

_____

_____

20 _____ _____

_____

_____

_____

20 _____ _____

_____

_____

_____

20 _____ _____

_____

_____

_____

*You, God, are awesome in your sanctuary; the God of Israel gives
power and strength to his people. Praise be to God! —Psalm 68:35*

**Father God, help me enjoy the craziness that can
be my home at times, and help me guide this child
of mine along the path that leads to You.**

25
April

In what ways have you become your own parents?

20 ___ _____

_____

_____

_____

20 ___ _____

_____

_____

_____

20 ___ _____

_____

_____

_____

20 ___ _____

_____

_____

_____

20 ___ _____

_____

_____

_____

You are a chosen people, a royal priesthood, a holy nation, God's special possession, that you may declare the praises of him who called you out of darkness into his wonderful light. —1 Peter 2:9

Father, it's a joy to be part of Your family. May that always be evident to those who know me.

The most surprised I've been recently as a mom was when _____.

26
April

20___ _____

_____

_____

20___ _____

_____

_____

20___ _____

_____

_____

20___ _____

_____

_____

20___ _____

_____

_____

The fear of the LORD is the beginning of knowledge; fools despise wisdom and instruction. —Proverbs 1:7 ESV

Lord of lords, please increase my wisdom, as I struggle to make the best decisions for my family.

27
April

"When I'm a mom, I'll never . . ." What rules of your own have you broken?

20 ___ _____

_____

_____

_____

20 ___ _____

_____

_____

_____

20 ___ _____

_____

_____

_____

20 ___ _____

_____

_____

_____

20 ___ _____

_____

_____

_____

Above all, my brothers, do not swear, either by heaven or by earth or by any other oath. —James 5:12 ESV

Forgive me, Lord, for any arrogance I have as a mom, and teach me to be constantly learning from those who have more experience than I do.

What bribes have you offered your kid?

20___

20___

20___

20___

20___

If you call out for insight and raise your voice for understanding,
. . . then you will understand the fear of the LORD and
find the knowledge of God. —*Proverbs 2:3; 5 ESV*

God, I desire to know You more than any earthly
treasure. Please make Yourself real to me today.

29
April

What blessing do you want to give your child?

20 ___ _____

_____

_____

_____

20 ___ _____

_____

_____

_____

20 ___ _____

_____

_____

_____

20 ___ _____

_____

_____

_____

20 ___ _____

_____

_____

_____

"The LORD bless you and keep you; the LORD make his face shine on you and be gracious to you; the LORD turn his face toward you and give you peace." —Numbers 6:24–26

Heavenly Father, bless this child of mine with all the richness of knowing and loving You.

*What's an adorable thing your
child says incorrectly?*

20 ___ _____

_____

_____

20 ___ _____

_____

_____

20 ___ _____

_____

_____

20 ___ _____

_____

_____

20 ___ _____

_____

_____

*You will walk in the way of the good and keep to the
paths of the righteous. —Proverbs 2:20*

God, please set Your angels around my child and guide them
along the path of the righteous every day of their life.

1
May

20 ___ _____

_____

_____

_____

20 ___ _____

_____

_____

_____

20 ___ _____

_____

_____

_____

20 ___ _____

_____

_____

_____

20 ___ _____

_____

_____

_____

*"Come to me, all who are weary and burdened, and
I will give you rest." —Matthew 11:28*

**Father, help me cherish each moment of today
while anticipating the summer days ahead.**

What traits do you see in your child that
remind you of a family member?

2
May

20___ _____

_____

_____

20___ _____

_____

_____

20___ _____

_____

_____

20___ _____

_____

_____

20___ _____

_____

_____

We, who are many, are one body in Christ, and individually
members one of another. —Romans 12:5 *NASB*

Lord, thank You for this addition to our family.
Help me teach my child Your loving ways.

3

May

What book does your child love most right now?

20___ _____

_____

_____

20___ _____

_____

_____

20___ _____

_____

_____

20___ _____

_____

_____

20___ _____

_____

_____

Faith comes by hearing, and hearing by the
word of God. —Romans 10:17 NKJV

Creator God, reveal the wonders of Your world to
my child through resources that honor You.

What is your favorite way to relax and recharge?

4
May

20 ___ _____

_____

_____

_____

20 ___ _____

_____

_____

_____

20 ___ _____

_____

_____

_____

20 ___ _____

_____

_____

_____

20 ___ _____

_____

_____

_____

Fear the LORD, and turn away from evil. It will be healing to your flesh and refreshment to your bones. —Proverbs 3:7–8 ESV

Lord, thank You for the time I have to relax and recharge— even if it's just momentary. Help me make the most of it.

5
May

How are you teaching your child God's Word?

20___ _____

_____

_____

_____

20___ _____

_____

_____

_____

20___ _____

_____

_____

_____

20___ _____

_____

_____

_____

20___ _____

_____

_____

_____

From infancy you have known the Holy Scriptures, which are able to make you wise for salvation through faith in Christ Jesus. —2 Timothy 3:15

Father, as I work to teach my child Your Word, please make it come alive in their soul.

How has your child changed the most
during this past school year?

6
May

20 ___ _____

_____

_____

_____

20 ___ _____

_____

_____

_____

20 ___ _____

_____

_____

_____

20 ___ _____

_____

_____

_____

20 ___ _____

_____

_____

_____

"I am leaving you with a gift—peace of mind and heart.
And the peace I give is a gift the world cannot give. So
don't be troubled or afraid." —John 14:27 NLT

Father, protect me from fear as I mother, and
remind me of the freedom I have in You.

7
May

My most effective method of disciplining my child right now is _____.

20___ _____
_____
_____
_____

20___ _____
_____
_____
_____

20___ _____
_____
_____
_____

20___ _____
_____
_____
_____

20___ _____
_____
_____
_____

The LORD disciplines those he loves, as a father the son he delights in. —Proverbs 3:12

God, give me wisdom as I raise my child to know when to be firm in discipline and when to extend grace.

What is the most challenging thing
about motherhood for you today?

8
May

20 ___

20 ___

20 ___

20 ___

20 ___

Blessed is the one who perseveres under trial. —James 1:12

Heavenly Father, though the day may be hard,
remind me that I do not go it alone.

9
May

A tradition I'd like to start for Mother's Day is:

20 ___ _____

20 ___ _____

20 ___ _____

20 ___ _____

20 ___ _____

Start children off on the way they should go, and even when they are old they will not turn from it. —Proverbs 22:6

Lord, please strengthen the heart of my child to grow faithful and to trust in You.

What is your child's favorite treat?

20 _____ _____

_____

_____

_____

20 _____ _____

_____

_____

_____

20 _____ _____

_____

_____

_____

20 _____ _____

_____

_____

_____

20 _____ _____

_____

_____

_____

*Fathers, do not exasperate your children; instead, bring them up
in the training and instruction of the Lord.* —Ephesians 6:4

**Gracious God, if I exasperate my child, help me to
see it immediately and apologize quickly.**

11
May

The sweetest thing my child has
given me recently is:

20 _____

20 _____

20 _____

20 _____

20 _____

Children are a gift from the LORD; they are a
reward from him. —Psalm 127:3 NLT

Father, thank You for the most precious gift of my
child. Help me steward that gift for Your glory.

Who is a mentor in your life right now?

12
May

20___

20___

20___

20___

20___

These older women must train the younger women to love their husbands and their children. —Titus 2:4 NLT

God, bring women who love You into my life, and help me be a faithful mentor to moms younger than I am as well.

13
May

What are you praying for your
child most often these days?

20___ _____
_____
_____
_____

20___ _____
_____
_____
_____

20___ _____
_____
_____
_____

20___ _____
_____
_____
_____

20___ _____
_____
_____
_____

But Jesus said, "Let the children come to me. Don't stop
them! For the Kingdom of Heaven belongs to those who
are like these children." —Matthew 19:14 NLT

Father God, no matter what happens in my child's life,
please always draw my child back to Your side.

*What are you looking forward to
this summer with your kids?*

14
May

20 ___ _____

_____

_____

_____

20 ___ _____

_____

_____

_____

20 ___ _____

_____

_____

_____

20 ___ _____

_____

_____

_____

20 ___ _____

_____

_____

_____

*Take care, and keep your soul diligently, lest you forget the
things that your eyes have seen, . . . Make them known to your
children and your children's children.* —Deuteronomy 4:9 ESV

**Father, thank You for the gift of a full life, and
for the joy of dreaming about our future.**

15
May

I am awestruck when my kid _____.

20___ _____

20___ _____

20___ _____

20___ _____

20___ _____

*Praise the name of God forever and ever, for he has
all wisdom and power.* —Daniel 2:20 NLT

**Eternal God, I praise You in advance for the
wondrous plans You have for my child.**

What is your child's favorite song right now?

20 __ _____

_____

_____

_____

20 __ _____

_____

_____

_____

20 __ _____

_____

_____

_____

20 __ _____

_____

_____

_____

20 __ _____

_____

_____

_____

*Oh come, let us sing to the LORD! Let us shout joyfully
to the Rock of our salvation. —Psalm 95:1 NKJV*

**Divine Father, I am grateful You have given us the
gift of song—to express both joy and sorrow.**

17
May

What did you receive for Mother's Day this year?

20___ _____

_____

_____

_____

20___ _____

_____

_____

_____

20___ _____

_____

_____

_____

20___ _____

_____

_____

_____

20___ _____

_____

_____

_____

*Lay up these words of mine in your heart and in your soul . . . You
shall teach them to your children.* —Deuteronomy 11:18–19 ESV

**Father, help me not to set my hopes unrealistically
high about traditions like Mother's Day, but to
celebrate the gift of salvation in You most of all.**

How has God been faithful to you lately?

18
May

20 ___ _____

20 ___ _____

20 ___ _____

20 ___ _____

20 ___ _____

*The father makes known to the children your
faithfulness.* —Isaiah 38:19 ESV

**God, open my child's eyes to see Your
faithfulness in their life every day.**

19
May

What's your favorite story to tell your child?

20___

20___

20___

20___

20___

Pass the story down from generation to generation. —Joel 1:3 NLT

Lord God, make the stories of Your goodness
be always present in my mind, so that I can tell
them to my child anytime, anywhere.

What is your child's favorite meal?

20 ___

20 ___

20 ___

20 ___

20 ___

*Turn my eyes away from worthless things; preserve my
life according to your word. —Psalm 119:37*

**Father, protect my heart from jealousy, my eyes from
covetousness, my lips from gossip, and my ears from
comparison. Focus me on Your Word instead.**

21
May

*What has been distracting you
from God's purposes lately?*

20 ___ _____

_____

_____

_____

20 ___ _____

_____

_____

_____

20 ___ _____

_____

_____

_____

20 ___ _____

_____

_____

_____

20 ___ _____

_____

_____

_____

*Set your minds on things above, not on
earthly things. —Colossians 3:2*

**God, You alone are worthy of our praise. Let
my life be a testimony to that truth.**

Today I'm going to set aside some time
to _____.

.

22

May

20 ___ _____

_____

_____

_____

20 ___ _____

_____

_____

_____

20 ___ _____

_____

_____

_____

20 ___ _____

_____

_____

_____

20 ___ _____

_____

_____

_____

"If you remain in me and my words remain in you, ask whatever
you wish, and it will be done for you." —John 15:7

**Dear Lord, thank You for Your Word and the opportunity
to grow in my knowledge and love of You through it.**

23
May

What makes your child laugh?

20 ___ _____

_____

_____

_____

20 ___ _____

_____

_____

_____

20 ___ _____

_____

_____

_____

20 ___ _____

_____

_____

_____

20 ___ _____

_____

_____

_____

He will once again fill your mouth with laughter and your lips with shouts of joy. —Job 8:21 NLT

Good Father, I treasure the laughter You bring to my child and the way it uplifts my spirit.

What makes you smile about your kid today?

24
May

20___ _____
_____
_____
_____

20___ _____
_____
_____
_____

20___ _____
_____
_____
_____

20___ _____
_____
_____
_____

20___ _____
_____
_____
_____

Serve the LORD your God with joy and enthusiasm for the abundant benefits you have received. —Deuteronomy 28:47 NLT

Father, fill me with the lightness of joy in You so that I may guide my family to be cheerful children of God.

25
May

What did your parents or grandparents teach you about following the Lord?

20 _____ _____

_____

_____

_____

20 _____ _____

_____

_____

_____

20 _____ _____

_____

_____

_____

20 _____ _____

_____

_____

_____

20 _____ _____

_____

_____

_____

Worship and serve him with your whole heart and a willing mind. —1 Chronicles 28:9 NLT

Father, I pray that my child would have a deep desire to know You through Your Word and that reading Scripture would be a daily call on my child's life.

How do you need to protect your heart this week?

26
May

20____ _____

20____ _____

20____ _____

20____ _____

20____ _____

Keep your heart with all vigilance, for from it flow the springs of life. —Proverbs 4:23 ESV

God, I know the overflow of my heart can be life-giving or life-stealing for my child. Help me be a fountain of grace in their life.

27
May

How do you need to show your child
some compassion right now?

20 ___ _____

_____

_____

_____

20 ___ _____

_____

_____

_____

20 ___ _____

_____

_____

_____

20 ___ _____

_____

_____

_____

20 ___ _____

_____

_____

_____

The LORD is like a father to his children, tender and
compassionate to those who fear him. —Psalm 103:13 NLT

Father, fill my heart with Your compassion for my child.
Help me know the best way to love my child.

What's something fun you can do with your child today to show your family you care?

28
May

20____

20____

20____

20____

20____

Those who won't care for their relatives, especially those in their own household, have denied the true faith. Such people are worse than unbelievers. —1 Timothy 5:8 NLT

Inspire me, Father, to love my family creatively, authentically, and meaningfully.

29
May

20 ___ _____

_____

_____

_____

20 ___ _____

_____

_____

_____

20 ___ _____

_____

_____

_____

20 ___ _____

_____

_____

_____

20 ___ _____

_____

_____

_____

He settles the childless woman in her home as a happy mother of children. Praise the LORD. —Psalm 113:9

All-knowing God, increase my creativity today to lead fun-filled activities for my child to enjoy.

Who is the biggest help to you
with your child right now?

30
May

20 ___ _____

_____

_____

_____

20 ___ _____

_____

_____

_____

20 ___ _____

_____

_____

_____

20 ___ _____

_____

_____

_____

20 ___ _____

_____

_____

_____

Therefore, as the elect of God, holy and beloved, put on tender mercies,
kindness, humility, meekness, longsuffering. —Colossians 3:12 NKJV

Faithful Lord, thank You for the family and friends You
have placed in my life to support me in motherhood.

31
May

Where do you go to become more peaceful?

20____ _____

20____ _____

20____ _____

20____ _____

20____ _____

"Peace I leave with you; my peace I give you. I do not give to you as the world gives. Do not let your hearts be troubled and do not be afraid." —John 14:27

Grant me moments of peace, Lord, in the midst of a phase of life that's full of unpredictability.

What inspires you about this time of year?

20 _____ _____

_____

_____

_____

20 _____ _____

_____

_____

_____

20 _____ _____

_____

_____

_____

20 _____ _____

_____

_____

_____

20 _____ _____

_____

_____

_____

Discipline your children, for in that there is hope. —Proverbs 19:18

Father, when my child's bad behavior discourages me,
remind me that there is hope in You—and that You continue
to love me faithfully when I fall into sinful patterns too.

2

June

20 ___ _____

_____

_____

_____

20 ___ _____

_____

_____

_____

20 ___ _____

_____

_____

_____

20 ___ _____

_____

_____

_____

20 ___ _____

_____

_____

_____

His anger lasts only a moment, but his favor lasts a lifetime; weeping may stay for the night, but rejoicing comes in the morning. —Psalm 30:5

God, the freedom I find in Your forgiveness is cause for rejoicing. Thank You for loving me fully.

What is one thing you will do today to honor your parents, or to help your child honor your spouse?

3
June

20____ _____

20____ _____

20____ _____

20____ _____

20____ _____

"Honor your father and your mother, that your days may be long in the land that the LORD your God is giving you." —Exodus 20:12 ESV

Father, even though I may not always agree with my parents, help me honor them in all I say and do.

4
June

20 ___

20 ___

20 ___

20 ___

20 ___

The LORD sees every heart and knows every plan and thought. If you seek him, you will find him. —1 Chronicles 28:9 NLT

Draw me ever closer to You, Lord. I seek to know You fully.

What do you most love about weekends?

20___ _____

_____

_____

20___ _____

_____

_____

20___ _____

_____

_____

20___ _____

_____

_____

20___ _____

_____

_____

*There is a special rest waiting for the people
of God. —Hebrews 4:9 NLT*

Prince of Peace, I pray that my child learns to play
well with others and extend compassion.

6
June

*What adjective would you use to
describe your child today?*

20___ _____

_____

_____

_____

20___ _____

_____

_____

_____

20___ _____

_____

_____

_____

20___ _____

_____

_____

_____

20___ _____

_____

_____

_____

I thank my God every time I remember you. —Philippians 1:3

**Gracious God, help me nurture my child's
talents and the unique gifts You give.**

Has your child made any new friends recently?

7

June

20____ _____

_____

_____

_____

20____ _____

_____

_____

_____

20____ _____

_____

_____

_____

20____ _____

_____

_____

_____

20____ _____

_____

_____

_____

*A friend loves at all times, and a brother is born
for adversity.* —Proverbs 17:17 NKJV

**Father, please teach my child how to be
a loving and faithful friend.**

8
June

What has changed most about you
since you've become a mom?

20 ___ _____

_____

_____

_____

20 ___ _____

_____

_____

_____

20 ___ _____

_____

_____

_____

20 ___ _____

_____

_____

_____

20 ___ _____

_____

_____

_____

This means that anyone who belongs to Christ has become a new person.
The old life is gone; a new life has begun! —2 Corinthians 5:17 NLT

Father, it's hard to shed all the habits of my old life, but
remind me every day that I am a new woman in You!

A tradition I'd like to start for Father's Day is:

9
June

20 ____

20 ____

20 ____

20 ____

20 ____

He will not let you stumble; the one who watches over you will not slumber. —Psalm 121:3 NLT

Lord God, when I try to do it all on my own, I fail. But when I let You lead me, I find rest.

10
June

What prayer has God answered for you lately?

20___ _____

_____

_____

_____

20___ _____

_____

_____

_____

20___ _____

_____

_____

_____

20___ _____

_____

_____

_____

20___ _____

_____

_____

_____

"You didn't choose me. I chose you. I appointed you to go and produce lasting fruit, so that the Father will give you whatever you ask for, using my name." —John 15:16 NLT

Father, thank You for listening to my prayers. Please grow the seeds of faith that I hope to plant in my child's heart.

What do you love about the city you live in?

20____

20____

20____

20____

20____

*You are no longer strangers and aliens, but you are fellow citizens with
the saints and members of the household of God. —Ephesians 2:19 ESV*

Father, You promise us a new Jerusalem is coming. Help me
spread Your light in the city I call home in the meantime.

12
June

How has your child lived up to the meaning of their name this week?

20 __ _____

_____

_____

_____

20 __ _____

_____

_____

_____

20 __ _____

_____

_____

_____

20 __ _____

_____

_____

_____

20 __ _____

_____

_____

_____

"Fear not, for I have redeemed you; I have called you by name, you are mine." —Isaiah 43:1 ESV

God, You knew Your plans for my child before they even had a name. Thank You for Your goodness and faithfulness.

What adventure have you taken
with your child recently?

13
June

20___

20___

20___

20___

20___

As far as the east is from the west, so far does he remove
our transgressions from us. —Psalm 103:12 ESV

Father, thank You for extending Your mercy toward me
to forgive my moments of failure as a mom. Guide me in
grace, that I may help point my child toward You.

14
June

What do you respect most about your husband?

20 ___

20 ___

20 ___

20 ___

20 ___

He must manage his own family well and see that his children obey him,
and he must do so in a manner worthy of full respect. —1 Timothy 3:4

Lord God, I desire to be the type of mother
who will be worthy of respect. Shape my heart,
that my child will recognize You in me.

*What encouraging word can you speak
to your family members today?*

15
June

20___ _____

_____

_____

_____

20___ _____

_____

_____

_____

20___ _____

_____

_____

_____

20___ _____

_____

_____

_____

20___ _____

_____

_____

_____

*Encourage each other and build each other up, just as
you are already doing.* —1 Thessalonians 5:11 NLT

**Father, keep any hurtful words from my mouth, and let me
speak only encouragement and blessing to my child.**

16
June

What did you give your husband for Father's Day?

20____ _____

20____ _____

20____ _____

20____ _____

20____ _____

For this child I prayed, and the Lᴏʀᴅ has granted me my petition that I made to him. —1 Samuel 1:27 ESV

Father, I'm so grateful for this amazing, curious, quirky, beautiful child. Thank You for letting me be a mother to them.

What do you want to ask God for
on your child's behalf?

20 ___ _____

_____

_____

20 ___ _____

_____

_____

20 ___ _____

_____

_____

20 ___ _____

_____

_____

20 ___ _____

_____

_____

Lift up your hands to Him for the life of your
little ones. —Lamentations 2:19 NASB

God, I will join You on the spiritual battlefield to fight for my
child's soul. Show me what I should be praying for them.

18
June

20 _____ _____

_____

_____

_____

20 _____ _____

_____

_____

_____

20 _____ _____

_____

_____

_____

20 _____ _____

_____

_____

_____

20 _____ _____

_____

_____

_____

*Discipline your children, and they will give you peace; they
will bring you the delights you desire. —Proverbs 29:17*

**Father, sometimes it's hard for me to stay consistent
in my discipline. Give me strength, resolve, and
wisdom as I parent this young child of Yours.**

*What big decision are you
praying over these days?*

19
June

20 _____

20 _____

20 _____

20 _____

20 _____

*"I am leaving you with a gift—peace of mind and heart.
And the peace I give is a gift the world cannot give.
So don't be troubled or afraid." —John 14:27* NLT

**Father, You know the plans You have for
me. Let me trust You in that.**

20
June

How has God been patient with you lately?

20 ___

20 ___

20 ___

20 ___

20 ___

The LORD is slow to anger and filled with unfailing love, forgiving every kind of sin and rebellion. —Numbers 14:18 NLT

Lord God, Your patience with me is a gift I do not deserve. Help me recognize it and let it spill over into my relationship with my child.

*What spiritual legacy do you hope
to leave for your child?*

21
June

20 ___ _____

_____

_____

_____

20 ___ _____

_____

_____

_____

20 ___ _____

_____

_____

_____

20 ___ _____

_____

_____

_____

20 ___ _____

_____

_____

_____

*He did what was pleasing in the LORD's sight, just as his
father, Amaziah, had done. —2 Chronicles 26:4 NLT*

**Lord, when my grandchildren and great-grandchildren
remember me, let my love for You be their strongest memory.**

22
June

What's worrying you right now?

20 _____ _____

20 _____ _____

20 _____ _____

20 _____ _____

20 _____ _____

Do not be anxious about anything, but in every situation, by prayer and petition, with thanksgiving, present your requests to God. —Philippians 4:6

Father, I claim the peace that passes all human understanding in my life, that my decisions and actions won't be based in fear but in complete confidence in You.

What's the best advice about
marriage you've been given?

23
June

20___ _____

_____

_____

_____

20___ _____

_____

_____

_____

20___ _____

_____

_____

_____

20___ _____

_____

_____

_____

20___ _____

_____

_____

_____

*Follow my advice, my son; always treasure
my commands.* —Proverbs 7:1 NLT

Father, marriage can be hard, but it is a gift from You.
Strengthen mine, so that it will be a blessing to our child.

24
June

What are you most hopeful about right now?

20___ _____

_____

_____

_____

20___ _____

_____

_____

_____

20___ _____

_____

_____

_____

20___ _____

_____

_____

_____

20___ _____

_____

_____

_____

Those who hope in the LORD will renew their strength. They will soar on wings like eagles; they will run and not grow weary, they will walk and not be faint. —Isaiah 40:31

Father, when the mundane tasks of motherhood wear me down, remind me of the hope You're calling me to.

What adventures would you like to go on?

25
June

20____

20____

20____

20____

20____

"Be strong and courageous. Do not be afraid; do not be discouraged, for the LORD your God will be with you wherever you go." —Joshua 1:9

Father, I want my child to know the courage and strength they can find in You. Give me a spirit of whimsy and adventure so they can see that more fully.

26
June

What do you find hardest about disciplining your child?

20 ___ _____

_____

_____

_____

20 ___ _____

_____

_____

_____

20 ___ _____

_____

_____

_____

20 ___ _____

_____

_____

_____

20 ___ _____

_____

_____

_____

A child left undisciplined disgraces its mother. —Proverbs 29:15

Father, let my child know Your love through my
steady hand of discipline and compassion.

A Fourth of July tradition I'd like to start is:

27
June

20___ _____

_____

_____

20___ _____

_____

_____

20___ _____

_____

_____

20___ _____

_____

_____

20___ _____

_____

_____

Ponder the path of your feet; then all your
ways will be sure. —Proverbs 4:26 ESV

Lord, keep me from impulsive, rash decisions.
Instead, help me and my husband think intentionally
about the plans our family makes.

28
June

As a wife, what do you want to improve on this week?

20 _____ _____

20 _____ _____

20 _____ _____

20 _____ _____

20 _____ _____

House and wealth are inherited from fathers, but a prudent wife is from the LORD. —**Proverbs 19:14** ESV

God, help me see ways I can be a blessing to my husband so that coming home is the highlight of his day.

How has God shown you His strength lately?

29
June

20____

20____

20____

20____

20____

*The name of the LORD is a fortified tower; the righteous
run to it and are safe. —Proverbs 18:10*

**Father, I praise you for Your strength and protection. Please
build Your strong tower of refuge around my family.**

30
June

What burdens are you helping carry for others right now?

20 ___ _____

_____

_____

_____

20 ___ _____

_____

_____

_____

20 ___ _____

_____

_____

_____

20 ___ _____

_____

_____

_____

20 ___ _____

_____

_____

_____

Cast your burden on the LORD, and he will sustain you; he will never permit the righteous to be moved. —Psalm 55:22 ESV

Prince of Peace, please come and make Your presence known among my friends who are suffering, that their sorrow will not be too much for them to bear.

*What is your favorite thing to do
with your kid that's free?*

1

July

20 ___ _____

_____

_____

_____

20 ___ _____

_____

_____

_____

20 ___ _____

_____

_____

_____

20 ___ _____

_____

_____

_____

20 ___ _____

_____

_____

_____

*Your ways are in full view of the LORD, and he
examines all your paths. —Proverbs 5:21*

**God, as You watch me parent this child, please reveal
any sinful habits I have developed as a mother.**

2
July

*What book are you reading
aloud to your child now?*

20 ___

20 ___

20 ___

20 ___

20 ___

*God is our refuge and strength, always ready to help in times
of trouble. So we will not fear. —Psalm 46:1-2 NLT*

**Father, so much about parenting is out of my
control, but protect me from turning to fear
instead of turning to You in those moments.**

What is your child's favorite birthday tradition?

3
July

20___

20___

20___

20___

20___

God has not given us a spirit of fear and timidity, but of power, love, and self-discipline. —2 Timothy 1:7 NLT

Lord God, move in my child's life in such a way that it will never be marked by fear but instead by Your power and love.

4
July

How did you celebrate the
Fourth of July this year?

20 ___ _____

_____

_____

_____

20 ___ _____

_____

_____

_____

20 ___ _____

_____

_____

_____

20 ___ _____

_____

_____

_____

20 ___ _____

_____

_____

_____

I have set the LORD always before me; because he is at my
right hand, I shall not be shaken. —Psalm 16:8 ESV

Hold me firmly, Lord, when life around
me seems to sway and shake.

In what ways has God been
setting you free lately?

5
July

20___ _____

_____

_____

20___ _____

_____

_____

20___ _____

_____

_____

20___ _____

_____

_____

20___ _____

_____

_____

*Cast your burden on the LORD, and he will sustain you; he will
never permit the righteous to be moved. —Psalm 55:22 ESV*

Lord, at times my burdens are too heavy to bear
alone. Thank You for taking them for me.

6
July

20 ___ _____

_____

_____

_____

20 ___ _____

_____

_____

_____

20 ___ _____

_____

_____

_____

20 ___ _____

_____

_____

_____

20 ___ _____

_____

_____

_____

I took my troubles to the LORD; I cried out to him, and
he answered my prayer. —Psalm 120:1 NLT

Father God, You hear me every time I call to You. Wrap
me in Your presence, so that I may hear You too.

What's your favorite way to serve your child?

7

July

20___ _____

20___ _____

20___ _____

20___ _____

20___ _____

The one thing I ask of the LORD—the thing I seek most—is to live in the house of the LORD all the days of my life, delighting in the LORD's perfections and meditating in his Temple. —Psalm 27:4 NLT

God, I ask that the desire to live in Your house and delight in Your perfection would be foremost in my child's heart.

8
July

What do you hope your child will be as an adult?

20 ___ _____

_____

_____

_____

20 ___ _____

_____

_____

_____

20 ___ _____

_____

_____

_____

20 ___ _____

_____

_____

_____

20 ___ _____

_____

_____

_____

*"Greater love has no one than this: to lay down
one's life for one's friends." —John 15:13*

**Father God, You are a friend to the friendless.
Teach my child to be the same.**

What family tradition do you want
to continue with your child?

9
July

20___ _____
_____
_____
_____

20___ _____
_____
_____
_____

20___ _____
_____
_____
_____

20___ _____
_____
_____
_____

20___ _____
_____
_____
_____

We know that God causes everything to work together for
the good of those who love God and are called according
to his purpose for them. —Romans 8:28 NLT

God, it's sometimes hard to see the fruit in my child's
life, but I cling to Your promise that it's coming!

10
July

20 _____ _____

20 _____ _____

20 _____ _____

20 _____ _____

20 _____ _____

Fathers, do not exasperate your children; instead, bring them up in the training and instruction of the Lord. —Ephesians 6:4

Lord God, let me be a source of encouragement and renewal for my child, never one of discouragement or frustration.

What makes your child laugh?

20 ___ _____

_____

_____

_____

20 ___ _____

_____

_____

_____

20 ___ _____

_____

_____

_____

20 ___ _____

_____

_____

_____

20 ___ _____

_____

_____

_____

*May the God of hope fill you with all joy and peace
in believing, so that by the power of the Holy Spirit
you may abound in hope. —Romans 15:13 ESV*

**God, there is darkness in this world, but please protect my
child's heart and fill it with the hope of Your promises.**

12
July

*What character quality do you
most value in your child?*

20 ___ _____

_____

_____

_____

20 ___ _____

_____

_____

_____

20 ___ _____

_____

_____

_____

20 ___ _____

_____

_____

_____

20 ___ _____

_____

_____

_____

*So that Christ may dwell in your hearts
through faith. —Ephesians 3:17 ESV*

**Author of Salvation, please make my child's
heart Your dwelling place. Fill my child with
an unending desire to know You.**

*What does your child share in
common with your husband?*

20 _____ _____

_____

_____

_____

20 _____ _____

_____

_____

_____

20 _____ _____

_____

_____

_____

20 _____ _____

_____

_____

_____

20 _____ _____

_____

_____

_____

*See what kind of love the Father has given to us, that we should
be called children of God; and so we are.* —1 John 3:1 ESV

**When I struggle as a mom, remind me to turn to
You—my perfect Father—for wisdom.**

14
July

Who is your child's favorite TV character?

20 ___ _____

_____

_____

_____

20 ___ _____

_____

_____

_____

20 ___ _____

_____

_____

_____

20 ___ _____

_____

_____

_____

20 ___ _____

_____

_____

_____

Let us hold tightly without wavering to the hope we affirm, for God can be trusted to keep his promise. —Hebrews 10:23 NLT

Father, there are times when I doubt. Make my heart steadfast to trust Your promises.

What is your child's favorite summer activity?

15
July

20___ _____

20___ _____

20___ _____

20___ _____

20___ _____

You know that when your faith is tested, your endurance
has a chance to grow. —James 1:3 NLT

God, let the difficult things I'm experiencing be
seeds of endurance and faith in my life.

16
July

What is the first thing your child does each day?

20____ _____

20____ _____

20____ _____

20____ _____

20____ _____

The LORD is my shepherd; I have all that I need. —Psalm 23:1 NLT

**When I get greedy for more, remind me, God, that
in You I have everything I will ever need.**

Where do you go to hide and get some me-time?

17
July

20___

20___

20___

20___

20___

Since we are surrounded by so great a cloud of witnesses, let us also lay aside every weight . . . and let us run with endurance the race that is set before us. —Hebrews 12:1 ESV

Father, show me the things I need to lay aside so that I can run my race with endurance.

18
July

If I were going to give my chid an award,
if would be for _____.

20___ _____
_____
_____
_____

20___ _____
_____
_____
_____

20___ _____
_____
_____
_____

20___ _____
_____
_____
_____

20___ _____
_____
_____
_____

What then shall we say to these things? If God is for
us, who can be against us? —Romans 8:31 ESV

God, You are for my child. Thank You for fighting for
them in a way that nothing can stand against You.

What is your child's favorite breakfast?

19
July

20___ _____

_____

_____

20___ _____

_____

_____

20___ _____

_____

_____

20___ _____

_____

_____

20___ _____

_____

_____

On the day I called, you answered me; my strength
of soul you increased. —Psalm 138:3 ESV

Father, please strengthen my soul—give me hope, faith,
courage, and anything else I'll need to bring You glory today.

20
July

What can you thank your child for today?

20 ____ _____

_____

_____

_____

20 ____ _____

_____

_____

_____

20 ____ _____

_____

_____

_____

20 ____ _____

_____

_____

_____

20 ____ _____

_____

_____

_____

Jesus looked at them and said, "With man this is impossible,
but with God all things are possible." —Matthew 19:26

God, You know the battles my child is fighting. Please fight
for my child, because with You anything is possible.

*What goal would you like to set for yourself
as the new school year begins soon?*

21
July

20____

20____

20____

20____

20____

I can do all this through him who gives me strength. —Philippians 4:13

**God, motherhood can make me weary. Please give
me the strength I need to love my child well.**

22
July

What parenting books have inspired you lately?

20____ _____

20____ _____

20____ _____

20____ _____

20____ _____

The God of heaven will set up a kingdom that will never be destroyed, nor will it be left to another people. —Daniel 2:44

Father, I praise You for Your unfailing goodness. Your kingdom will last forever, and I get to be part of it. Thank You!

What's the last thing that made you cry?

23
July

20 ___ _____

20 ___ _____

20 ___ _____

20 ___ _____

20 ___ _____

For the LORD your God is living among you. He is a mighty savior. He will take delight in you with gladness. With his love, he will calm all your fears. He will rejoice over you with joyful songs. —*Zephaniah 3:17* NLT

Oh, Father, I long to hear the joyful songs You sing over me. Let me hear Your voice today.

24
July

How are you different from most of the other mothers in your social group?

20 _____ _____

20 _____ _____

20 _____ _____

20 _____ _____

20 _____ _____

So be strong and courageous, all you who put your hope in the LORD! —Psalm 31:24 NLT

My hope is in You, God. You alone are holy and good. Thank You for loving me.

What habit do you have that drives
your child or spouse crazy?

25
July

20___ _____

_____

_____

20___ _____

_____

_____

20___ _____

_____

_____

20___ _____

_____

_____

20___ _____

_____

_____

"Well done, my good and faithful servant. You have been
faithful in handling this small amount, so now I will give
you many more responsibilities." —Matthew 25:21 NLT

Father, I pray that when my time is up, You'll declare
these words over me and celebrate with me too.

26
July

When have you said "yes" to your
child that you later regretted?

20 ___ _____
_____
_____
_____

20 ___ _____
_____
_____
_____

20 ___ _____
_____
_____
_____

20 ___ _____
_____
_____
_____

20 ___ _____
_____
_____
_____

*"What no eye has seen, what no ear has heard, and what
no human mind has conceived"—the things God has
prepared for those who love him. —1 Corinthians 2:9*

**Father, I praise Your goodness. I can't even comprehend
how cool the place You've prepared for me is. Thank You!**

What is the last birthday present you received?

20 ___ _____

20 ___ _____

20 ___ _____

20 ___ _____

20 ___ _____

*Taste and see that the LORD is good; blessed is the
one who takes refuge in him. —Psalm 34:8*

**I've seen Your goodness in my life, Lord.
Continue to show Yourself to me.**

28
July

What's the hardest thing about being a mom?

20 ___ _____

_____

_____

_____

20 ___ _____

_____

_____

_____

20 ___ _____

_____

_____

_____

20 ___ _____

_____

_____

_____

20 ___ _____

_____

_____

_____

Blessed is the one who does not walk in step with the wicked or stand in the way that sinners take or sit in the company of mockers. —Psalm 1:1

Father, protect my child from the way of the wicked. Instead, guide my child along Your paths of righteousness.

What's your favorite part of the day?

29
July

20___ _____

20___ _____

20___ _____

20___ _____

20___ _____

But the Lord stood with me and gave me strength. —2 Timothy 4:17 NLT

**God, You stand with me. When I think I can't take
another step, remind me of this truth.**

30
July

Who is loving you well right now?

20 ___ _____

_____

_____

_____

20 ___ _____

_____

_____

_____

20 ___ _____

_____

_____

_____

20 ___ _____

_____

_____

_____

20 ___ _____

_____

_____

_____

Everyone who thus hopes in him purifies himself as he is pure. —1 John 3:3 ESV

Father, fill me with hope for You, and purify me of all unrighteousness.

Who do you turn to for advice?

20 ___ _____

20 ___ _____

20 ___ _____

20 ___ _____

20 ___ _____

He will wipe away every tear from their eyes, and death shall be no more, neither shall there be mourning, nor crying, nor pain anymore, for the former things have passed away. —Revelation 21:4 ESV

Father, there's crying in my house almost daily. Thank You for Your promise that one day this will be no more.

1
August

What's your favorite verse about parenting?

20 ___ _____

_____

_____

_____

20 ___ _____

_____

_____

_____

20 ___ _____

_____

_____

_____

20 ___ _____

_____

_____

_____

20 ___ _____

_____

_____

_____

"Choose my instruction instead of silver, knowledge rather than choice gold, for wisdom is more precious than rubies, and nothing you desire can compare with her." —Proverbs 8:10–11

Father God, give me wisdom. I cannot parent this child well alone; I need You!

What has motherhood caused
you to give up in life?

2
August

20_____

20_____

20_____

20_____

20_____

For Christ's sake, I delight in weaknesses, in insults, in
hardships, in persecutions, in difficulties. For when I am
weak, then I am strong. —2 Corinthians 12:10

Father, I see Your strength so clearly when I am weak. Thank
You for being perfect for my child in the moments when I fail.

3
August

*Have you been brokenhearted
over anything lately?*

20___ _____

_____

_____

_____

20___ _____

_____

_____

_____

20___ _____

_____

_____

_____

20___ _____

_____

_____

_____

20___ _____

_____

_____

_____

*He heals the brokenhearted and binds up
their wounds. —Psalm 147:3 ESV*

**Father God, I've been wounded by relationships in my past.
Heal me so that I don't pass those wounds on to my child.**

What is your child's favorite thing
to do with their grandparents?

4

August

20 ___ _____

_____

_____

_____

20 ___ _____

_____

_____

_____

20 ___ _____

_____

_____

_____

20 ___ _____

_____

_____

_____

20 ___ _____

_____

_____

_____

God settles the solitary in a home; he leads out the prisoners to
prosperity, but the rebellious dwell in a parched land. —Psalm 68:6 ESV

God, Your desire is for everyone to be in
a family. Thank You for mine.

5

August

What's your favorite way to serve your husband?

20____ _____

_____

_____

20____ _____

_____

_____

20____ _____

_____

_____

20____ _____

_____

_____

20____ _____

_____

_____

Then I will know everything completely, just as God now knows me completely. —1 Corinthians 13:12 NLT

Lord, I can't see the big picture of what You're doing in my child's life yet, but I trust Your goodness and Your plan for them.

What do you worry about at night?

20___

20___

20___

20___

20___

*Let us come boldly to the throne of our gracious God.
There we will receive his mercy, and we will find grace to
help us when we need it most. —Hebrews 4:16 NLT*

**Father, I come boldly to Your throne asking
for grace. You know I need it.**

7
August

How has God been a refuge for you?

20 ___ _____

20 ___ _____

20 ___ _____

20 ___ _____

20 ___ _____

The LORD is good, a strong refuge when trouble comes. He is close to those who trust in him. —Nahum 1:7 NLT

God, when trouble comes, remind me to run to You as my refuge. You will be close to me there.

Where is your child's favorite
place to play in your house?

8

August

20 ___

20 ___

20 ___

20 ___

20 ___

We get knocked down, but we are not destroyed. —2 Corinthians 4:9 NLT

Father God, I feel like I'm knocked down so often, but in Your
grace I'm not destroyed. Thank You for being there for me.

9

August

20_____

20_____

20_____

20_____

20_____

*"Have I not commanded you? Be strong and courageous.
Do not be afraid; do not be discouraged, for the LORD your
God will be with you wherever you go." —Joshua 1:9*

**Lord God, there is joy in the fact that I can find courage
in You. Thank You for the thrill of adventure.**

What's one absolute splurge you wish
you could have right now?

20 ___ _____

20 ___ _____

20 ___ _____

20 ___ _____

20 ___ _____

This same God who takes care of me will supply all your
needs from his glorious riches, which have been given
to us in Christ Jesus. —Philippians 4:19 NLT

**Father, thank You for loving my child so much that You
are taking care of their each and every need.**

11
August

Who is your (or your child's) most faithful friend?

20 ___ _____

20 ___ _____

20 ___ _____

20 ___ _____

20 ___ _____

The faithful love of the LORD never ends! His mercies never cease. Great is his faithfulness. —Lamentations 3:22–23 NLT

Motherhood can be hard, Father, but I'm encouraged by the new mercies I experience every morning in You.

What seems impossible in your life right now?

12
August

20___ _____

20___ _____

20___ _____

20___ _____

20___ _____

Jesus looked at them and said, "With man it is impossible, but not with God. For all things are possible with God." —Mark 10:27 ESV

Lord, my mountain of to-dos can seem overwhelming at times. Give me focus and wisdom, to know when to work and when to rest.

13
August

What has been a big encouragement to you lately?

20 ___ _____

_____

_____

_____

20 ___ _____

_____

_____

_____

20 ___ _____

_____

_____

_____

20 ___ _____

_____

_____

_____

20 ___ _____

_____

_____

_____

Encourage one another and build each other up, just as in fact you are doing. —1 Thessalonians 5:11

Father, please send words of encouragement my way today, and give me a chance to pass them on to my child or someone else.

*What do you wear around the house
when you want to relax?*

20____ _____

_____

_____

_____

20____ _____

_____

_____

_____

20____ _____

_____

_____

_____

20____ _____

_____

_____

_____

20____ _____

_____

_____

_____

Comfort, comfort my people, says your God. —Isaiah 40:1 ESV

**God, Your desire is for my heart to be comforted.
Thank You for that tender mercy.**

15
August

What's a big act of generosity someone has done for you?

20___ _____

20___ _____

20___ _____

20___ _____

20___ _____

"Since you are precious and honored in my sight, and because I love you, I will give people in exchange for you, nations in exchange for your life." —Isaiah 43:4

Father, make me more aware of You, and more grateful for Your love.

*What's the most enjoyable part
of being a mother?*

16
August

20____ _____

_____

_____

_____

20____ _____

_____

_____

_____

20____ _____

_____

_____

_____

20____ _____

_____

_____

_____

20____ _____

_____

_____

_____

*The God of all comfort, who comforts us in all our troubles,
so that we can comfort those in any trouble with the comfort
we ourselves receive from God. —2 Corinthians 1:3–4*

**Father, open my eyes to the needs of others around me, and
give me compassion to comfort the brokenhearted.**

17
August

What are you hoping for?

20 ___ _____

_____

_____

_____

20 ___ _____

_____

_____

_____

20 ___ _____

_____

_____

_____

20 ___ _____

_____

_____

_____

20 ___ _____

_____

_____

_____

Be strong and take heart, all you who hope in the LORD. —Psalm 31:24

Father, my hope is in You. I have no reason to be discouraged . . . ever!

What's your biggest pet peeve?

20 ___

20 ___

20 ___

20 ___

20 ___

Our light and momentary troubles are achieving for us an
eternal glory that far outweighs them all. —2 Corinthians 4:17

God, when I am overwhelmed by the things
that don't go right in my day, remind me that
these are light and momentary troubles.

19
August

20____ _____

20____ _____

20____ _____

20____ _____

20____ _____

May the favor of the LORD our God rest on us; establish the work of our hands for us—yes, establish the work of our hands. —Psalm 90:17

Father, grant Your favor to me as I am pouring my heart and soul into shaping this little child to be the best possible person they can be.

Which of your neighbors do you turn to when you need help, or just a friend?

20
August

20 ___ _____

_____

_____

_____

20 ___ _____

_____

_____

_____

20 ___ _____

_____

_____

_____

20 ___ _____

_____

_____

_____

20 ___ _____

_____

_____

_____

Each of us should please our neighbors for their good, to build them up. —Romans 15:2

God, help me be a good neighbor to those living near me, as well as those I encounter on social media.

21
August

What does your child do to honor you?

20___

20___

20___

20___

20___

"Honor your father and your mother, as the LORD your God commanded you, that your days may be long, and that it may go well with you in the land that the LORD your God is giving you." —Deuteronomy 5:16 ESV

Father, give my child a desire to honor their parents, not for my benefit, but for theirs.

*How does being a mother push you
out of your comfort zone?*

22

August

20___ _____

20___ _____

20___ _____

20___ _____

20___ _____

*The LORD himself goes before you and will be with you;
he will never leave you nor forsake you. Do not be afraid;
do not be discouraged. —Deuteronomy 31:8*

**God, no matter what this journey of parenting brings,
You will be right here with me going through it all too.**

23
August

What are you doing to give back right now?

20___

20___

20___

20___

20___

If the willingness is there, the gift is acceptable according to what one has, not according to what one does not have. —2 Corinthians 8:12

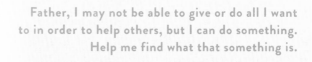

Father, I may not be able to give or do all I want to in order to help others, but I can do something. Help me find what that something is.

What is your child's favorite season?

24
August

20 ___ _____

_____

_____

_____

20 ___ _____

_____

_____

_____

20 ___ _____

_____

_____

_____

20 ___ _____

_____

_____

_____

20 ___ _____

_____

_____

_____

*Humble yourselves, therefore, under the mighty hand of God
so that at the proper time he may exalt you, casting all your
anxieties on him, because he cares for you. —1 Peter 5:6–7 ESV*

**Lord, I humble myself before You. Direct
my paths today. I will follow You.**

25
August

*What is your child's favorite
thing to say right now?*

20 ___ _____

_____

_____

_____

20 ___ _____

_____

_____

_____

20 ___ _____

_____

_____

_____

20 ___ _____

_____

_____

_____

20 ___ _____

_____

_____

_____

*Don't be afraid; you are more valuable to God than
a whole flock of sparrows. —Matthew 10:31 NLT*

**Father, I love to hear the words that come from
my child's mouth. They are so precious. Remind
me that You love to hear from me too.**

Who has made you feel good this week? Why?

26
August

20___ _____

_____

_____

_____

20___ _____

_____

_____

_____

20___ _____

_____

_____

_____

20___ _____

_____

_____

_____

20___ _____

_____

_____

_____

I can do all this through him who gives
me strength. —Philippians 4:13

Father, thank You for the small
encouragements You give me each day.

27
August

Do you plan to travel with your child as they grow? Where do you hope to visit?

20 ___

20 ___

20 ___

20 ___

20 ___

We are citizens of heaven, where the Lord Jesus Christ lives. And we are eagerly waiting for him to return as our Savior. —Philippians 3:20 NLT

Come, Lord Jesus! I long for the day when my family and I will see You face-to-face in all Your glory. Thank You for loving us.

What makes you the most exhausted?

28
August

20____

20____

20____

20____

20____

Jesus said, "Come to me, all of you who are weary and carry heavy burdens, and I will give you rest." —Matthew 11:28 NLT

Father, please give me pockets of rest today, when I can reflect on the promises You give to me.

29
August

*How are you planning to celebrate
Labor Day this year?*

20 ___ _____

_____

_____

_____

20 ___ _____

_____

_____

_____

20 ___ _____

_____

_____

_____

20 ___ _____

_____

_____

_____

20 ___ _____

_____

_____

_____

*For the LORD watches over the path of the godly, but the path
of the wicked leads to destruction.* —Psalm 1:6 NLT

**Holy God, please set my child on the path of the
godly. Rescue my child, and draw them to You.**

How has God shown you His grace lately?

30
August

20 _____ _____

_____

_____

20 _____ _____

_____

_____

20 _____ _____

_____

_____

20 _____ _____

_____

_____

20 _____ _____

_____

_____

The grace of the Lord Jesus be with you. —1 Corinthians 16:23 ESV

**God, I know You extend Your grace
to me. Help me receive it.**

31
August

What are you hiding from?

20_____ _____

_____

_____

_____

20_____ _____

_____

_____

_____

20_____ _____

_____

_____

_____

20_____ _____

_____

_____

_____

20_____ _____

_____

_____

_____

You are my hiding place and my shield; I hope in your word. —Psalm 119:114 ESV

Father, show me the things that distract me from keeping Your commandments, especially as they relate to my role as mother.

What inspires you about this time of year?

1
September

20___

20___

20___

20___

20___

Let us consider how we may spur one another on toward love and good deeds. —Hebrews 10:24

Father, what are some creative ways I can spur my child on to love and good deeds?

2
September

20 _____ _____

_____

_____

_____

20 _____ _____

_____

_____

_____

20 _____ _____

_____

_____

_____

20 _____ _____

_____

_____

_____

20 _____ _____

_____

_____

_____

*And so, Lord, where do I put my hope? My only
hope is in you.* —Psalm 39:7 NLT

**God, show me the places in my life where I'm
putting my hope in things other than You.**

What work inspires you, excites you, and is fun for you to do?

3
September

20 _____ _____

_____

_____

_____

20 _____ _____

_____

_____

_____

20 _____ _____

_____

_____

_____

20 _____ _____

_____

_____

_____

20 _____ _____

_____

_____

_____

Therefore, my dear brothers and sisters, stand firm. Let nothing move you. Always give yourselves fully to the work of the Lord, because you know that your labor in the Lord is not in vain. —1 Corinthians 15:58

Father, help me not to be distracted with my child, but to give myself fully to the work of mothering my child well.

4
September

20___

20___

20___

20___

20___

While we look forward with hope to that wonderful day when the glory of our great God and Savior, Jesus Christ, will be revealed. —Titus 2:13 NLT

God, show me the places in my child's life where they need Your hope, and help me direct my child to You there.

Motherhood isn't a sprint, it's a marathon.
Where have you needed endurance lately?

5
September

20___ _____

20___ _____

20___ _____

20___ _____

20___ _____

May the God who gives endurance and encouragement
give you the same attitude of mind toward each
other that Christ Jesus had. —Romans 15:5

Father, as I look at my family today, help
me see them with Your eyes.

6
September

What Bible story has your child learned lately?

20____ _____

20____ _____

20____ _____

20____ _____

20____ _____

All Scripture is breathed out by God and profitable for teaching, . . . that the man of God may be complete, equipped for every good work. —2 Timothy 3:16–17 ESV

God, where do I need correction in my life? Lead me to an understanding, through Your Word.

What funny thing has your child said lately?

7

September

20____ _____

20____ _____

20____ _____

20____ _____

20____ _____

I will instruct you and teach you in the way you should go; I will counsel you with my loving eye on you. —Psalm 32:8

Father, thank You for not leaving me to figure out this life all on my own. Help me listen to You.

8
September

Whom have you been praying for lately?

20 _____ _____

20 _____ _____

20 _____ _____

20 _____ _____

20 _____ _____

*Rejoice in our confident hope. Be patient in trouble,
and keep on praying. —Romans 12:12 NLT*

**Father, help me always find joy in Your truth, no
matter what's happening in my life.**

Where do you love to take your child to play?

9
September

20 ___ _____

_____

_____

_____

20 ___ _____

_____

_____

_____

20 ___ _____

_____

_____

_____

20 ___ _____

_____

_____

_____

20 ___ _____

_____

_____

_____

O LORD, you alone are my hope. I've trusted you, O
LORD, from childhood. —Psalm 71:5 NLT

Oh, God, I ask that my child may be able to say, when
they're an adult, that they've trusted You since childhood.

10
September

What are you looking forward to about this fall with your child?

20___ _____

20___ _____

20___ _____

20___ _____

20___ _____

Be on your guard; stand firm in the faith; be courageous; be strong. —1 Corinthians 16:13

Father, protect my child with spiritual armor as my child stands firm in their faith.

*Whom do you have playdates
with most frequently?*

20 ___ _____

20 ___ _____

20 ___ _____

20 ___ _____

20 ___ _____

For the word of God will never fail. —Luke 1:37 NLT

**God, Your Word is true and good all the time.
Remind me of that when I doubt.**

12
September

How often are you able to get away for date nights with your spouse?

20 ___ _____

20 ___ _____

20 ___ _____

20 ___ _____

20 ___ _____

May God our Father and the Lord Jesus Christ give you grace and peace. —2 Corinthians 1:2 NLT

Father, fill my child with Your grace and Your peace. Let my child cast aside any fear or anxiety that's troubling them.

What news story has been dominating the headlines lately?

13
September

20____ _____

20____ _____

20____ _____

20____ _____

20____ _____

"Look among the nations, and see; wonder and be astounded. For I am doing a work in your days that you would not believe if told." —Habakkuk 1:5 ESV

Father, help me have a bigger perspective than just my own experience as I try to understand Your work in the world.

14
September

How has God done more than you imagined lately?

20 _____ _____

_____

_____

_____

20 _____ _____

_____

_____

_____

20 _____ _____

_____

_____

_____

20 _____ _____

_____

_____

_____

20 _____ _____

_____

_____

_____

Now to him who is able to do far more abundantly than all that we ask or think, according to the power at work within us. —Ephesians 3:20 ESV

God, Your will for my life may be far bigger than what I've imagined. Make my vision align with Yours.

What have you been dreaming and planning for ages, but haven't gotten around to actually doing?

15
September

20 _____ _____

_____

_____

20 _____ _____

_____

_____

20 _____ _____

_____

_____

20 _____ _____

_____

_____

20 _____ _____

_____

_____

All hard work brings a profit, but mere talk leads only to poverty. —Proverbs 14:23

Lord God, allow me to see a glimpse of the profit that will come from the work I put into raising my child.

16
September

Whom do you need to forgive,
or ask forgiveness from?

20____ _____

20____ _____

20____ _____

20____ _____

20____ _____

Esau . . . asked, "Who are these people with you?"
"These are the children God has graciously given to me,
your servant," Jacob replied. —Genesis 33:5 NLT

Father, I pray that every day my child will know how much
You love them, and that You think of my child as a gift.

Write down a memory from your child's birthday.

17
September

20 ___

20 ___

20 ___

20 ___

20 ___

He gives the childless woman a family, making her a happy mother. Praise the LORD! —Psalm 113:9 NLT

Father God, You've given me a family through the gift of this child. Praise You!

18
September

On what issues are you the most stubborn?

20 ___ _____

_____

_____

_____

20 ___ _____

_____

_____

_____

20 ___ _____

_____

_____

_____

20 ___ _____

_____

_____

_____

20 ___ _____

_____

_____

_____

I am asking you to respond as if you were my own children.
Open your hearts to us! —2 Corinthians 6:13 NLT

Lord, help me open my heart to my child every day, and please,
Father, allow my child to open their heart to me too.

What has your child recently
taught you about Christ?

19
September

20 _____ _____

_____

_____

_____

20 _____ _____

_____

_____

_____

20 _____ _____

_____

_____

_____

20 _____ _____

_____

_____

_____

20 _____ _____

_____

_____

_____

*"Out of the mouth of infants and nursing babies you
have prepared praise." —Matthew 21:16 ESV*

Holy God, I long for my child to know and love You.
Please put praise for You in my child's mouth.

20
September

Does your child have any bedtime fears?

20 ___

20 ___

20 ___

20 ___

20 ___

You keep him in perfect peace whose mind is stayed on you, because he trusts in you. —Isaiah 26:3 ESV

Father, despite the many distractions in my day, keep my mind stayed on You.

How is your child making an impact for Jesus on the people around them?

21
September

20___ _____

20___ _____

20___ _____

20___ _____

20___ _____

Out of the mouth of babies and infants, you have established strength because of your foes, to still the enemy and the avenger. —Psalm 8:2 ESV

God, establish Your strength in my family, through the mouth of my child. Amen!

22
September

What podcasts or TV shows is your child following right now?

20 ___ _____

20 ___ _____

20 ___ _____

20 ___ _____

20 ___ _____

*"See that you do not despise one of these little ones.
For I tell you that their angels in heaven always see the
face of my Father in heaven." —Matthew 18:10*

God, I praise You for Your great protection.

What is your child's favorite beverage?

23
September

20___ _____

_____

_____

_____

20___ _____

_____

_____

_____

20___ _____

_____

_____

_____

20___ _____

_____

_____

_____

20___ _____

_____

_____

_____

Like newborn babies, crave pure spiritual milk, so that by it you may grow up in your salvation, now that you have tasted that the Lord is good. —1 Peter 2:2–3

Father, please let my child crave Your Word, and through it develop a deep, true love for You.

24
September

What is your child good about obeying?

20___

20___

20___

20___

20___

Children, obey your parents in everything, for this
pleases the Lord. —Colossians 3:20

When my child obeys me, Lord, it pleases You.
Let my child feel Your delight in them.

What brings you the most joy about your child?

25

September

20 _____ _____

_____

_____

_____

20 _____ _____

_____

_____

_____

20 _____ _____

_____

_____

_____

20 _____ _____

_____

_____

_____

20 _____ _____

_____

_____

_____

I could have no greater joy than to hear that my children are following the truth. —3 John 1:4 NLT

Oh, Father, I ask that my child would walk in Your truth every day of their life.

26
September

20 _____ _____

_____

_____

_____

20 _____ _____

_____

_____

_____

20 _____ _____

_____

_____

_____

20 _____ _____

_____

_____

_____

20 _____ _____

_____

_____

_____

*Then God blessed them and said, "Be fruitful
and multiply." —Genesis 1:28 NLT*

God, my child is the greatest work of my life but also Your great
blessing on me. Thank You for the gift of being a mother.

*What new skill have you taught
your child recently?*

27
September

20 ___ _____

_____

_____

_____

20 ___ _____

_____

_____

_____

20 ___ _____

_____

_____

_____

20 ___ _____

_____

_____

_____

20 ___ _____

_____

_____

_____

*"I will teach all your children, and they will enjoy
great peace." —Isaiah 54:13 NLT*

**Lord, help me be faithful to teach my child Your Word
so my child knows You and knows peace.**

28
September

What is frustrating you or driving you crazy lately?

20 _____

20 _____

20 _____

20 _____

20 _____

"I have told you these things, so that in me you may have peace. In this world you will have trouble. But take heart! I have overcome the world." —John 16:33

Father, when I fear the darkness in this world, remind me that You have overcome it already!

*What's your favorite thing to do
after your child goes to bed?*

29
September

20 ___ _____

_____

_____

_____

20 ___ _____

_____

_____

_____

20 ___ _____

_____

_____

_____

20 ___ _____

_____

_____

_____

20 ___ _____

_____

_____

_____

*God our Father . . . never changes or casts a
shifting shadow. —James 1:17 NLT*

**Father, my child changes constantly—almost every day.
But You never change, and that is a great comfort to me.**

30
September

What is the last thing you argued about?

20 ___ _____

20 ___ _____

20 ___ _____

20 ___ _____

20 ___ _____

This is my comfort in my affliction, that your promise gives me life. —Psalm 119:50 ESV

God, when I'm weary and discouraged as a mom, please lead me to Your Word that gives me life.

What's your favorite way for your
family to show you they love you?

1
October

20 ___ _____

20 ___ _____

20 ___ _____

20 ___ _____

20 ___ _____

We have been unfaithful to our God . . . But in spite of
this, there is still hope for Israel. —Ezra 10:2

Father, I'll never be perfect as a mom, but I'm thankful
that my child has a perfect Father in You.

2
October

If you could take your child anywhere in the world on vacation, where would it be?

20___ _____

_____

_____

_____

20___ _____

_____

_____

_____

20___ _____

_____

_____

_____

20___ _____

_____

_____

_____

20___ _____

_____

_____

_____

"Whoever receives one such child in my name receives me, and whoever receives me, receives not me but him who sent me." —Mark 9:37 ESV

God, I'm reminded of the song lyric that to love another person is to see Your face. Thank You that, when I love my child, I'm loving You as well.

What do you do for self-care right now?

3
October

20___ _____

20___ _____

20___ _____

20___ _____

20___ _____

But [the Lord] does not excuse the guilty. He lays the sins of the parents upon their children; the entire family is affected—even children in the third and fourth generations. —Numbers 14:18 NLT

Lord, make clear to me the impact my sin really has. May that inspire me to follow Your law more closely.

4
October

How often do you and your husband get a date night?

20 _____ _____

_____

_____

_____

20 _____ _____

_____

_____

_____

20 _____ _____

_____

_____

_____

20 _____ _____

_____

_____

_____

20 _____ _____

_____

_____

_____

While he was yet a boy, he began to seek the God of David his father. —2 Chronicles 34:3 ESV

Lord God, I long for this to be said of my child, that they sought You from the time they were a small child too.

What is your child's favorite lunch food?

5
October

20___ _____

20___ _____

20___ _____

20___ _____

20___ _____

"When a woman is giving birth, she has sorrow because her hour has come, but when she has delivered the baby, she no longer remembers the anguish, for joy that a human being has been born into the world." —John 16:21 ESV

God, the experience of birthing a child is a miracle—a tiny expression of Your power and creativity.

6
October

What is your child's favorite word (or expression) to say right now?

20___ _____

20___ _____

20___ _____

20___ _____

20___ _____

Don't let anyone look down on you because you are young, but set an example for the believers in speech, in conduct, in love, in faith and in purity. —1 Timothy 4:12

Father, don't let me underestimate what my child can handle, and let me give them the freedom to set an example for others.

How does your child push your buttons?

7
October

20 _____ _____

_____

_____

_____

20 _____ _____

_____

_____

_____

20 _____ _____

_____

_____

_____

20 _____ _____

_____

_____

_____

20 _____ _____

_____

_____

_____

You will be secure, because there is hope; you will look about you and take your rest in safety. —Job 11:18

Father, as the evening hours shorten, let my family gather together at night around Your Word and find our hope there.

8
October

What skill are you so ready for your child to master right now?

20___ _____

_____

_____

20___ _____

_____

_____

20___ _____

_____

_____

20___ _____

_____

_____

20___ _____

_____

_____

Direct your children onto the right path, and when they are older, they will not leave it. —Proverbs 22:6 NLT

Oh, Father, I pray that my child will always stay on Your path, that they will love Your Word, and that they will seek to do what is right.

Who gives you the best parenting
advice at this stage?

9
October

20 ___ _____

_____

_____

20 ___ _____

_____

_____

20 ___ _____

_____

_____

20 ___ _____

_____

_____

20 ___ _____

_____

_____

*Then all the people went away to eat and drink, to send portions of
food and to celebrate with great joy, because they now understood
the words that had been made known to them. —Nehemiah 8:12*

**Father, as we come up on the holiday season soon, give me
a spirit of celebration because Your Word actually is true.**

10
October

What parenting issue do you and your husband disagree on right now?

20___ _____

20___ _____

20___ _____

20___ _____

20___ _____

Now to him who is able to do far more abundantly than all that we ask or think, according to the power at work within us, to him be glory . . . forever and ever. Amen. —Ephesians 3:20–21 ESV

Father, I praise Your holy name because You do abundantly more than I could ever dream. You are good, O God.

In what area has God given you
the gift of peace lately?

11
October

20_____ _____

_____

20_____ _____

_____

20_____ _____

_____

20_____ _____

_____

20_____ _____

_____

*"I am leaving you with a gift—peace of mind and heart.
And the peace I give is a gift the world cannot give. So
don't be troubled or afraid." —John 14:27 NLT*

Father, when things are going well with my child, help
me remember that peace is a gift from You too.

12
October

What's your favorite meal to cook for your family?

20_____ _____

20_____ _____

20_____ _____

20_____ _____

20_____ _____

You formed my inward parts; You wove me in my mother's womb. —Psalm 139:13 NASB

You created my child perfectly, Father, and I thank You for the gift of their life.

What's your go-to outfit of choice these days?

20 ___ _____

_____

_____

_____

20 ___ _____

_____

_____

_____

20 ___ _____

_____

_____

_____

20 ___ _____

_____

_____

_____

20 ___ _____

_____

_____

_____

*"If you remain in me and my words remain in you, ask whatever
you wish, and it will be done for you." —John 15:7*

God, I ask that my child would always remain in You and
that Your Word would always remain in my child.

14
October

What new skill do you want to learn?

20 ___ _____

20 ___ _____

20 ___ _____

20 ___ _____

20 ___ _____

Set your minds on things above, not on earthly things. —Colossians 3:2

Father, when I become overwhelmed with bottles and diapers and playdates, remind me to think about Your glory.

*How can your family spend time
serving others in need?*

15
October

20 _____ _____

_____

_____

_____

20 _____ _____

_____

_____

_____

20 _____ _____

_____

_____

_____

20 _____ _____

_____

_____

_____

20 _____ _____

_____

_____

_____

*A friend loves at all times, and a brother is born
for adversity.* —Proverbs 17:17 NKJV

**Father, I know my child will face adversity in
their life, but please give them friends who love
You and who will stick close in those times.**

16
October

Who's been a big encouragement to you lately?

20___ _____

_____

_____

_____

20___ _____

_____

_____

_____

20___ _____

_____

_____

_____

20___ _____

_____

_____

_____

20___ _____

_____

_____

_____

*Encourage each other and build each other up, just as
you are already doing. —1 Thessalonians 5:11 NLT*

God, please let every word that comes from my mouth
today be one that encourages and builds up my child.

Where can you cut back on some
of your household spending?

17
October

20 ___

20 ___

20 ___

20 ___

20 ___

The peace of God, which transcends all understanding, will guard
your hearts and your minds in Christ Jesus. —Philippians 4:7

God, I give my fears over to You and ask that You would
please replace them with Your perfect peace.

18
October

*Have you made any commitments
lately that you regret?*

20 _____ _____

_____

_____

_____

20 _____ _____

_____

_____

_____

20 _____ _____

_____

_____

_____

20 _____ _____

_____

_____

_____

20 _____ _____

_____

_____

_____

*Ponder the path of your feet; then all your
ways will be sure.* —Proverbs 4:26 ESV

Father, please give me wisdom to consider the
decisions we are making for our family to know
if they are aligned with Your will for us.

What's the hardest thing about
parenting right now?

19
October

20 _____ _____

_____

_____

_____

20 _____ _____

_____

_____

_____

20 _____ _____

_____

_____

_____

20 _____ _____

_____

_____

_____

20 _____ _____

_____

_____

_____

*For your ways are in full view of the LORD, and he
examines all your paths. —Proverbs 5:21*

God, You see every part of my life. Reveal to me
any part that isn't bringing glory to You.

20
October

Who do you want to become better friends with?

20 ____ _____

_____

_____

_____

20 ____ _____

_____

_____

_____

20 ____ _____

_____

_____

_____

20 ____ _____

_____

_____

_____

20 ____ _____

_____

_____

_____

"Greater love has no one than this: to lay down one's life for one's friends." —John 15:13

God, thank You for good friends—for my child and for me— who will drop everything and come when we need help.

What seemingly impossible goals (or, just, desires) have you set for yourself?

21
October

20 _____ _____

_____

_____

_____

20 _____ _____

_____

_____

_____

20 _____ _____

_____

_____

_____

20 _____ _____

_____

_____

_____

20 _____ _____

_____

_____

_____

Jesus looked at them and said, "With man this is impossible, but with God all things are possible." —Matthew 19:26

Do not let me be discouraged, God, because with You all things are possible.

22
October

Are you satisfied with your physical fitness?

20 ___ _____

_____

_____

_____

20 ___ _____

_____

_____

_____

20 ___ _____

_____

_____

_____

20 ___ _____

_____

_____

_____

20 ___ _____

_____

_____

_____

The Lord stood with me and gave me strength. —2 Timothy 4:17 NLT

**Father, when my strength to love my kid well is failing,
come stand with me and give me strength.**

What makes you happy?

23
October

20 ___ _____

_____

_____

_____

20 ___ _____

_____

_____

_____

20 ___ _____

_____

_____

_____

20 ___ _____

_____

_____

_____

20 ___ _____

_____

_____

_____

Delight yourself in the LORD, and he will give you the
desires of your heart. —Psalm 37:4 ESV

Lord God, I ask that You alone would be the desire of my
heart, and that my heart would be full of You.

24
October

What is your family doing to serve God?

20 ___ _____

_____

_____

_____

20 ___ _____

_____

_____

_____

20 ___ _____

_____

_____

_____

20 ___ _____

_____

_____

_____

20 ___ _____

_____

_____

_____

But as for me and my household, we will
serve the LORD. —Joshua 24:15

Father, please let my child always desire to serve You,
and help me direct them toward that in all they do.

*What do you feel like you're
a slave to right now?*

25
October

20____ _____

20____ _____

20____ _____

20____ _____

20____ _____

*For freedom Christ has set us free; stand firm therefore, and do
not submit again to a yoke of slavery. —Galatians 5:1 ESV*

**God, let me give up those things that take
me away from serving You well.**

26
October

20 _____

20 _____

20 _____

20 _____

20 _____

*My God will meet all your needs according to the riches
of his glory in Christ Jesus. —Philippians 4:19*

**Father, there is no need I have that You have not met.
Please fill me with contentment and gratitude daily.**

In what aspect of your life do you feel like you've gained the respect of others?

27
October

20 ___ _____

20 ___ _____

20 ___ _____

20 ___ _____

20 ___ _____

A gracious woman gains respect, but ruthless men gain only wealth. —Proverbs 11:16 NLT

Father, when I'm tempted to fight back or get angry, fill me with Your grace so that I may bring You glory.

28
October

What lesson did your parents teach you that's most applicable to you now, at this stage of your life?

20 ___ _____

_____

_____

_____

20 ___ _____

_____

_____

_____

20 ___ _____

_____

_____

_____

20 ___ _____

_____

_____

_____

20 ___ _____

_____

_____

_____

My son, keep your father's command and do not forsake your mother's teaching. Bind them always on your heart; fasten them around your neck. —Proverbs 6:20–21

God, help me find creative ways to speak Your Scripture into my child's life throughout the day.

What upcoming event are you
most excited about?

29
October

20 ___ _____

_____

_____

_____

20 ___ _____

_____

_____

_____

20 ___ _____

_____

_____

_____

20 ___ _____

_____

_____

_____

20 ___ _____

_____

_____

_____

For the LORD your God is living among you. He is a mighty savior. He
will take delight in you with gladness. With his love, he will calm all your
fears. He will rejoice over you with joyful songs. —Zephaniah 3:17 NLT

God, let my child experience the delight of
You rejoicing over them in song.

30
October

What could you do to make your mother (or a mother-type figure in your life) be glad today?

20 ___ _____

_____

_____

_____

20 ___ _____

_____

_____

_____

20 ___ _____

_____

_____

_____

20 ___ _____

_____

_____

_____

20 ___ _____

_____

_____

_____

Let your father and mother be glad; let her who bore you rejoice. —Proverbs 23:25 ESV

Father, help me recall the wonderful moments with my child, and let the frustrations fall away from my memory, so that I may be glad.

Did your child dress up in a costume this year? If so, as what?

31
October

20____ _____

_____

_____

_____

20____ _____

_____

_____

_____

20____ _____

_____

_____

_____

20____ _____

_____

_____

_____

20____ _____

_____

_____

_____

I praise you because I am fearfully and wonderfully made; your works are wonderful, I know that full well. —Psalm 139:14

God, thank You for giving us fun experiences and good friends in this life. They are reminders of Your goodness.

1
November

What's the craziest thing you all do as a family?

20 _____

20 _____

20 _____

20 _____

20 _____

For God is working in you, giving you the desire and the power to do what pleases him. —Philippians 2:13 NLT

Father, fill me with the desire to please You all throughout my day.

How do you hope to enjoy the cold winter weather with your child this year?

2
November

20____ _____

20____ _____

20____ _____

20____ _____

20____ _____

Remembering before our God and Father your work of faith and labor of love and steadfastness of hope in our Lord Jesus Christ. —1 Thessalonians 1:3 ESV

God, let my hope in You be unwavering, and let it spill over into my child's life as well.

3
November

*What's one word you would use to
describe your marriage right now?*

20 ___

20 ___

20 ___

20 ___

20 ___

*Those who hope in the LORD will renew their strength. They
will soar on wings like eagles; they will run and not grow
weary, they will walk and not be faint. —Isaiah 40:31*

**Father, I feel weary a lot these days. Please let
my hope in You renew my spirit.**

*What seems to be your child's
preferred love language?*

4
November

20___ _____

_____

_____

_____

20___ _____

_____

_____

_____

20___ _____

_____

_____

_____

20___ _____

_____

_____

_____

20___ _____

_____

_____

_____

"Be still, and know that I am God." —Psalm 46:10 ESV

God, help me find moments to be still and
reflect on Your goodness and holiness.

5
November

20____ _____

_____

_____

_____

20____ _____

_____

_____

_____

20____ _____

_____

_____

_____

20____ _____

_____

_____

_____

20____ _____

_____

_____

_____

Don't try to impress others. Be humble, thinking of others as better than yourselves. —Philippians 2:3 NLT

Father, the comparison game is so hard as a mom. Help me remember my child is Yours and I need to compare them to no one.

What do you think your child will
do for a living as an adult?

6
November

20____ _____

_____

_____

_____

20____ _____

_____

_____

_____

20____ _____

_____

_____

_____

20____ _____

_____

_____

_____

20____ _____

_____

_____

_____

He gives power to the weak and strength to
the powerless. —Isaiah 40:29 NLT

Father, when I feel weak please give me Your
strength to love my child well.

1
November

20____ _____

_____

_____

_____

20____ _____

_____

_____

_____

20____ _____

_____

_____

_____

20____ _____

_____

_____

_____

20____ _____

_____

_____

_____

From the ends of the earth I call to you, I call as my heart grows
faint; lead me to the rock that is higher than I. —Psalm 61:2

When I try to rely on my own strength, Lord, I will
fail. So lead me every day to You, my Rock.

The biggest mess my child has made lately is:

8
November

20 _____ _____

20 _____ _____

20 _____ _____

20 _____ _____

20 _____ _____

"Don't be afraid; you are more valuable to God than a whole flock of sparrows." —Matthew 10:31 NLT

Father, let me never forget how valuable I am—and my child is—to You.

9
November

My child's favorite activity or game is:

20___

20___

20___

20___

20___

Put all your hope in the gracious salvation that will come to you when Jesus Christ is revealed to the world. —1 Peter 1:13 NLT

Lord God, bring it to my attention when I put my hope in earthly things, and redirect me to You instead.

A tradition I'd like to start for Thanksgiving is:

10
November

20___ _____

20___ _____

20___ _____

20___ _____

20___ _____

"Heaven and earth will pass away, but my words
will not pass away." —Matthew 24:35 ESV

God, it's so easy to worry about my kid, but
remind me that You have an eternal plan for them
that's so much greater than what I see.

11
November

How often do you find time for yourself—to read a book or relax?

20 _____ _____

20 _____ _____

20 _____ _____

20 _____ _____

20 _____ _____

Though he slay me, yet will I hope in him. —Job 13:15

Father, Your plans for my child may not align with my plans. Lead me gently, Father, if that is the case.

*Who's the first person you'd call if you had
free time to go out to lunch or dinner?*

12
November

20 _____ _____

_____

_____

_____

20 _____ _____

_____

_____

_____

20 _____ _____

_____

_____

_____

20 _____ _____

_____

_____

_____

20 _____ _____

_____

_____

_____

*Guide me in your truth and teach me, for you are God my
Savior, and my hope is in you all day long. —Psalm 25:5*

**God, please let Your truth sink deep into
my soul so that I really learn it.**

13
November

*What would be a fun date night
for you and your child?*

20 _____ _____

_____

_____

_____

20 _____ _____

_____

_____

_____

20 _____ _____

_____

_____

_____

20 _____ _____

_____

_____

_____

20 _____ _____

_____

_____

_____

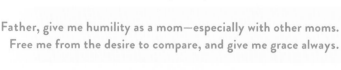

*No, O people, the LORD has told you what is good, and this
is what he requires of you: to do what is right, to love mercy,
and to walk humbly with your God. —Micah 6:8 NLT*

**Father, give me humility as a mom—especially with other moms.
Free me from the desire to compare, and give me grace always.**

*What are you most looking forward to
eating at Thanksgiving this year?*

14
November

20____ _____

_____

_____

_____

20____ _____

_____

_____

_____

20____ _____

_____

_____

_____

20____ _____

_____

_____

_____

20____ _____

_____

_____

_____

"For this is how God loved the world: He gave his one
and only Son, so that everyone who believes in him will
not perish but have eternal life." —John 3:16 NLT

**Oh, Father, I pray that my child will believe the good news
that Your one and only Son has given—the gift of eternal life.**

15
November

How does your family plan to give back over the Thanksgiving holiday?

20 ___ _____

20 ___ _____

20 ___ _____

20 ___ _____

20 ___ _____

"There is hope for your descendants," declares the LORD. —Jeremiah 31:17

Lord, because I strive to mold my child's heart for You, this promise brings me so much joy.

*What sermon, Bible study, or podcast
has impacted you spiritually?*

16
November

20 _____ _____

_____

_____

_____

20 _____ _____

_____

_____

_____

20 _____ _____

_____

_____

_____

20 _____ _____

_____

_____

_____

20 _____ _____

_____

_____

_____

*No discipline is enjoyable while it is happening—it's painful!
But afterward there will be a peaceful harvest of right living
for those who are trained in this way. —Hebrews 12:11 NLT*

**God, keep me strong when my kid begs not to be disciplined. I
know they don't like it, but it's making them understand Your truth.**

17
November

What is your child's favorite comfort item?

20 ___

20 ___

20 ___

20 ___

20 ___

God is our merciful Father and the source of all comfort. —2 Corinthians 1:3 NLT

God, when I'm sad and struggling, You comfort me. Thank You for Your compassion.

What is your greatest strength as a mom?

20___ _____

20___ _____

20___ _____

20___ _____

20___ _____

What is your mother? A lioness among lions! She lay down among the young lions and reared her cubs. —Ezekiel 19:2 NLT

Father, thank You for making me a woman who can be strong, powerful, and yet gentle with her child. Remind me of the strength You give me when I need it most.

19
November

How are you planning to celebrate
Thanksgiving this year?

20___ _____

_____

_____

20___ _____

_____

_____

20___ _____

_____

_____

20___ _____

_____

_____

20___ _____

_____

_____

God of Israel, may those who seek you not be put
to shame because of me. —Psalm 69:6

Father, when I fail my child, please protect
their heart and their love for You.

What are you most thankful for in your family?

20
November

20 ___ _____

_____

_____

_____

20 ___ _____

_____

_____

_____

20 ___ _____

_____

_____

_____

20 ___ _____

_____

_____

_____

20 ___ _____

_____

_____

_____

Even if my father and mother abandon me, the LORD will hold me close. —Psalm 27:10 NLT

Father, I'm awestruck by the truth that—as deeply and fully as I love my child—You love them even more.

21
November

What are you most looking forward to about Thanksgiving?

20 _____ _____

_____

_____

_____

20 _____ _____

_____

_____

_____

20 _____ _____

_____

_____

_____

20 _____ _____

_____

_____

_____

20 _____ _____

_____

_____

_____

Have you forgotten the encouraging words God spoke to you as his children? He said, "My child, don't make light of the LORD's discipline, and don't give up when he corrects you." —Hebrews 12:5 NLT

God, I ask that through my attitude toward my child, my child would view discipline as an opportunity to learn.

What are you dreading about Thanksgiving?

22
November

20___ _____

_____

_____

_____

20___ _____

_____

_____

_____

20___ _____

_____

_____

_____

20___ _____

_____

_____

_____

20___ _____

_____

_____

_____

"I will comfort you there in Jerusalem as a mother comforts her child." —Isaiah 66:13 NLT

Father, give me wisdom to see when my child needs to be comforted, and let that love be a reflection of Your care for them.

23
November

My child's biggest dream is to:

20 _____

20 _____

20 _____

20 _____

20 _____

Yes, you have been with me from birth; from my mother's womb you have cared for me. No wonder I am always praising you! —Psalm 71:6 NLT

God, You've been with me from the time I was in my mother's womb. Thank You for Your faithfulness!

How has God protected you lately?

24
November

20____

20____

20____

20____

20____

We wait in hope for the LORD; he is our help and our shield. —Psalm 33:20

God, You cover me with Your shield, to protect me from any attack. Praise You for Your strength and goodness!

25
November

What is your favorite compliment you give your child?

20 ___

20 ___

20 ___

20 ___

20 ___

You have comforted me by speaking so kindly to me. —Ruth 2:13 NLT

Oh, God, give me grace to speak kindly to
my child, even when it's not easy.

Where could you use more discretion in your life?

26
November

20____ _____

_____

_____

_____

20____ _____

_____

_____

_____

20____ _____

_____

_____

_____

20____ _____

_____

_____

_____

20____ _____

_____

_____

_____

*Discretion is a life-giving fountain to those
who possess it. —Proverbs 16:22 NLT*

**Father, don't let me get carried away by the parenting fads
and trends, but let my life be marked by discretion.**

27
November

When I was growing up, my mother loved to:

20 ___ _____

20 ___ _____

20 ___ _____

20 ___ _____

20 ___ _____

Your mother was like a vine planted by the water's edge. It had lush, green foliage because of the abundant water. —Ezekiel 19:10 NLT

Father, give me time to care for myself so that I can be that well-watered plant that nourishes my child.

The funniest thing my child has said recently was:

28

November

20____ _____

_____

_____

_____

20____ _____

_____

_____

_____

20____ _____

_____

_____

_____

20____ _____

_____

_____

_____

20____ _____

_____

_____

_____

He will tend his flock like a shepherd; he will gather the
lambs in his arms; he will carry them in his bosom, and gently
lead those that are with young. —Isaiah 40:11 ESV

Oh, Father, You gently lead mothers of young children.
Thank You so much for that promise.

29
November

*What's one word you would use to
describe your child right now?*

20 ___ _____
_____
_____
_____

20 ___ _____
_____
_____
_____

20 ___ _____
_____
_____
_____

20 ___ _____
_____
_____
_____

20 ___ _____
_____
_____
_____

*How beautiful upon the mountains are the feet of him
who brings good news. —Isaiah 52:7 ESV*

**Father, as I enter the Advent season with my family, help
us meditate on Your Word throughout every day.**

*What are you most looking forward
to this winter with your kids?*

30
November

20 ___ _____

_____

_____

20 ___ _____

_____

_____

20 ___ _____

_____

_____

20 ___ _____

_____

_____

20 ___ _____

_____

_____

*The LORD God said to the serpent . . . "I will put enmity between you
and the woman, and between your offspring and her offspring; he shall
bruise your head, and you shall bruise his heel."* —Genesis 3:14–15 ESV

**Father, I feel the effects of the serpent in my life, but
I give You praise for defeating him in the end.**

1
December

What Advent or Christmas traditions are most special to you?

20___ _____

20___ _____

20___ _____

20___ _____

20___ _____

And the glory of the LORD will be revealed, and all people will see it together. —Isaiah 40:5

Oh, Lord, I long to see Your glory alongside my child. Reveal Yourself to us.

What is your child hoping to receive for Christmas?

2
December

20 _____ _____

_____

_____

_____

20 _____ _____

_____

_____

_____

20 _____ _____

_____

_____

_____

20 _____ _____

_____

_____

_____

20 _____ _____

_____

_____

_____

*Abram believed the LORD, and he credited it to
him as righteousness. —Genesis 15:6*

**Father, give us faith to believe Your good news. I claim the
righteousness of Christ for myself and my family.**

3
December

20___ _____

20___ _____

20___ _____

20___ _____

20___ _____

*"I myself will call to account anyone who does not listen to my words
that the prophet speaks in my name." —Deuteronomy 18:19*

**Oh, Father, humble me and convict my heart over the places
in my life where I do not heed the words of Your prophets.**

What holiday recipes are you most
excited to make (or eat) this year?

4
December

20____ _____

_____

_____

_____

20____ _____

_____

_____

_____

20____ _____

_____

_____

_____

20____ _____

_____

_____

_____

20____ _____

_____

_____

_____

*I will sing of the LORD's unfailing love forever! Young and old will
hear of your faithfulness. Your unfailing love will last forever. Your
faithfulness is as enduring as the heavens. —Psalm 89:1–4 NLT*

**Lord, Your love never, ever, ever fails. You
are always good. Thank You.**

5
December

20___

20___

20___

20___

20___

In that day the wolf and the lamb will live together; the leopard will lie down with the baby goat. The calf and the yearling will be safe with the lion, and a little child will lead them all. —Isaiah 11:6 NLT

I long for the day, Lord, when I might parent my child with no fear. Thank You for the promise of Your eternal kingdom.

A tradition I'd like to start for Christmas is:

20 ____ _____

_____

_____

_____

20 ____ _____

_____

_____

_____

20 ____ _____

_____

_____

_____

20 ____ _____

_____

_____

_____

20 ____ _____

_____

_____

_____

But you, O Bethlehem Ephrathah, are only a small village . . . Yet a
ruler of Israel . . . will come from you on my behalf. —Micah 5:2 NLT

God, remind me that You do mighty works in small people and
places. Don't let me underestimate Your ability to use my child.

7

December

What is your child's favorite Christmas carol?

20___ _____

_____

_____

_____

20___ _____

_____

_____

_____

20___ _____

_____

_____

_____

20___ _____

_____

_____

_____

20___ _____

_____

_____

_____

"It is he who shall build the temple of the LORD and shall bear royal honor, and shall sit and rule on his throne." —Zechariah 6:13 ESV

Father, don't let me forget the fact that peace with You is a tremendous gift that Jesus gave us.

What is your child's favorite
Christmas decoration?

8
December

20 _____ _____

_____

_____

_____

20 _____ _____

_____

_____

_____

20 _____ _____

_____

_____

_____

20 _____ _____

_____

_____

_____

20 _____ _____

_____

_____

_____

"For I the LORD do not change; therefore you, O children
of Jacob, are not consumed." —Malachi 3:6 ESV

God, my child has a hope and a future because You are
perfect and holy. Thank You a million times.

9
December

20 _____

20 _____

20 _____

20 _____

20 _____

*In the beginning was the Word, and the Word was with
God, and the Word was God.* —John 1:1 ESV

**God, let Your Word be the center of my household and
the first place we turn when we need help.**

What are you dreading about Christmas?

20____ _____

_____

_____

_____

20____ _____

_____

_____

_____

20____ _____

_____

_____

_____

20____ _____

_____

_____

_____

20____ _____

_____

_____

_____

*The true light that gives light to everyone was
coming into the world. —John 1:9*

**Father, thank You for bringing us light so that we don't
have to raise our child in darkness, not knowing You.**

11
December

How do you celebrate the Advent season?

20 _____ _____

_____

_____

_____

20 _____ _____

_____

_____

_____

20 _____ _____

_____

_____

_____

20 _____ _____

_____

_____

_____

20 _____ _____

_____

_____

_____

Prepare the way for the Lord, make straight paths for him. —Mark 1:3

**God, help me realize my job as a mother is to prepare
the way for You to work in my child's life.**

What's the worst thing about the holidays?

12
December

20 ___ _____

_____

_____

_____

20 ___ _____

_____

_____

_____

20 ___ _____

_____

_____

_____

20 ___ _____

_____

_____

_____

20 ___ _____

_____

_____

_____

*The angel said, "Don't be afraid, Zechariah! God has
heard your prayer. Your wife, Elizabeth, will give you a son,
and you are to name him John." —Luke 1:13 NLT*

**Remind me, holy Lord, that my child really belongs
to You. Reveal to me Your will for my child.**

13
December

20 _____ _____

_____

_____

_____

20 _____ _____

_____

_____

_____

20 _____ _____

_____

_____

_____

20 _____ _____

_____

_____

_____

20 _____ _____

_____

_____

_____

He will turn the hearts of the fathers to their children, and he will cause those who are rebellious to accept the wisdom of the godly. —Luke 1:17 NLT

Oh, Father, I pray that my child's relationship with their earthly father will be strong and full of love.

What is your favorite holiday
memory with your child?

14
December

20 __ _____

_____

_____

_____

20 __ _____

_____

_____

_____

20 __ _____

_____

_____

_____

20 __ _____

_____

_____

_____

20 __ _____

_____

_____

_____

"How kind the Lord is!" [Elizabeth] exclaimed. "He has taken
away my disgrace of having no children." —Luke 1:25 NLT

God, the opportunity to be a mother is such a gift. Help
me appreciate it when I feel tired and overwhelmed.

15
December

*What do you hope to teach your child
about Jesus' birth this year?*

20 _____

20 _____

20 _____

20 _____

20 _____

*You are blessed because you believed that the Lord
would do what he said. —Luke 1:45 NLT*

**Lord, thank You for the gift of believing in You. I pray that
You would capture the heart of my child by that belief too.**

What makes you hopeful this time of year?

16
December

20___ _____

_____

_____

_____

20___ _____

_____

_____

_____

20___ _____

_____

_____

_____

20___ _____

_____

_____

_____

20___ _____

_____

_____

_____

He who is mighty has done great things for me,
and holy is his name. —Luke 1:49 ESV

Father, as I reflect on the Christmas story, I'm humbled
by the great length You went to in order to give me life.

17
December

20 ___

20 ___

20 ___

20 ___

20 ___

All who heard them laid them up in their hearts, saying, "What then will this child be?" For the hand of the Lord was with him. —Luke 1:66 ESV

God, just as Your hand was with John the Baptist, please also be with my child so that they may do great things for You.

What's the favorite gift you're giving this season?

18
December

20 ___

20 ___

20 ___

20 ___

20 ___

Blessed be the Lord God of Israel, for he has visited and redeemed his people. —Luke 1:68 ESV

Lord, I praise You for Your goodness to save me from my sin. It's so humbling. Thank You.

19
December

The Lord has encouraged me recently by:

20 _____ _____

_____

_____

_____

20 _____ _____

_____

_____

_____

20 _____ _____

_____

_____

_____

20 _____ _____

_____

_____

_____

20 _____ _____

_____

_____

_____

"I will not ask, and I will not put the LORD to the test." —Isaiah 7:12 ESV

God, give me the energy and desire to seek You and find You in Your Word.

What about the Christmas story is
especially meaningful to you this year?

20
December

20 ___ _____

_____

_____

_____

20 ___ _____

_____

_____

_____

20 ___ _____

_____

_____

_____

20 ___ _____

_____

_____

_____

20 ___ _____

_____

_____

_____

"Do not be afraid, Mary; you have found favor with God. You will conceive
and give birth to a son, and you are to call him Jesus." —Luke 1:30–31

Father, I can't imagine the emotions that swirled in Mary's
heart. I praise You for her faithfulness to You.

21
December

Jesus is called Wonderful Counselor, Mighty God, Everlasting Father . . . What is your favorite name for Him right now?

20 _____ _____

_____

_____

_____

20 _____ _____

_____

_____

_____

20 _____ _____

_____

_____

_____

20 _____ _____

_____

_____

_____

20 _____ _____

_____

_____

_____

For to us a child is born, to us a son is given, and the government will be on his shoulders. And he will be called Wonderful Counselor, Mighty God, Everlasting Father, Prince of Peace. —Isaiah 9:6

God, help me reinforce for my child that this holiday season is about Your power and goodness more than gifts and treats.

How can you set aside the busyness and really focus on Christ this week?

22
December

20____ _____

20____ _____

20____ _____

20____ _____

20____ _____

"He will save his people from their sins." —Matthew 1:21

Father, the true gift we received this year is salvation from our sins. Help my child to understand that deeply.

23
December

*What's your favorite way to worship
God this time of year?*

20 ___ _____

20 ___ _____

20 ___ _____

20 ___ _____

20 ___ _____

*Glory to God in highest heaven, and peace on earth to
those with whom God is pleased.* —Luke 2:14 NLT

**Oh, Father, I long for You to be pleased with my
little family. Thank You for loving us.**

*What did you say when you tucked
your child in on Christmas Eve?*

24
December

20____ _____

_____

_____

_____

20____ _____

_____

_____

_____

20____ _____

_____

_____

_____

20____ _____

_____

_____

_____

20____ _____

_____

_____

_____

*Where is the newborn king of the Jews? We saw his star as it
rose, and we have come to worship him. —Matthew 2:2 NLT*

**Thank You, Father, for coming to save us. Please
lead me in worshipping You this Christmas.**

25
December

What was your child's favorite
Christmas gift this year?

20 _____ _____

20 _____ _____

20 _____ _____

20 _____ _____

20 _____ _____

*I have seen your salvation, which you have prepared
for all people.* —Luke 2:30–31 NLT

**Lord God, I praise You for Your great
gift that none of us deserves.**

How will you find ways to serve
God in the new year?

26
December

20___ _____

_____

_____

_____

20___ _____

_____

_____

_____

20___ _____

_____

_____

_____

20___ _____

_____

_____

_____

20___ _____

_____

_____

_____

Fear the LORD and serve him in sincerity and
in faithfulness. —Joshua 24:14 ESV

God, let my child's love for You be evident in the way
they serve others sincerely and faithfully.

27
December

20 ___ _____

_____

_____

_____

20 ___ _____

_____

_____

_____

20 ___ _____

_____

_____

_____

20 ___ _____

_____

_____

_____

20 ___ _____

_____

_____

_____

Now let your unfailing love comfort me, just as you
promised me, your servant. —Psalm 119:76 NLT

Father, as we settle back into the post-holiday routine,
fill our hearts and our house with love for You.

What resolutions do you have for the next year, to make sure you continue to walk in God's path?

28
December

20____ —————————————————————————

20____ —————————————————————————

20____ —————————————————————————

20____ —————————————————————————

20____ —————————————————————————

Your steadfast love is before my eyes, and I walk in your faithfulness. —Psalm 26:3 ESV

God, protect my child from the trap of greed and covetousness, and let them instead see only Your love.

29
December

20 ___ _____
_____
_____
_____

20 ___ _____
_____
_____
_____

20 ___ _____
_____
_____
_____

20 ___ _____
_____
_____
_____

20 ___ _____
_____
_____
_____

*In the morning, Lord, you hear my voice; in the morning I lay
my requests before you and wait expectantly.* —Psalm 5:3

**God, I trust You with my child and my family, and I treasure
my time talking with You. Thank You for loving us well.**

What's the best thing that happened
to your child this year?

30
December

20___ _____

_____

_____

20___ _____

_____

_____

20___ _____

_____

_____

20___ _____

_____

_____

20___ _____

_____

_____

Hope deferred makes the heart sick, but a longing
fulfilled is a tree of life. —Proverbs 13:12

Father, as I look ahead to a new year, please fulfill the
desires that make my heart ache, according to Your will.

31
December

What is your dream for your family next year?

20___ _____

20___ _____

20___ _____

20___ _____

20___ _____

"For I know the plans I have for you," declares the LORD, "plans to prosper you and not to harm you, plans to give you hope and a future." —Jeremiah 29:11

Father, I'm excited to learn what You have in store for my child this year. I praise You for Your faithfulness to us.

My Favorite Bible Verses

My Favorite Bible Verses

My Favorite Bible Verses

My Favorite Bible Verses

My Favorite Bible Verses

My Favorite Bible Verses

Notes

Notes

Notes

Notes

Notes

Notes